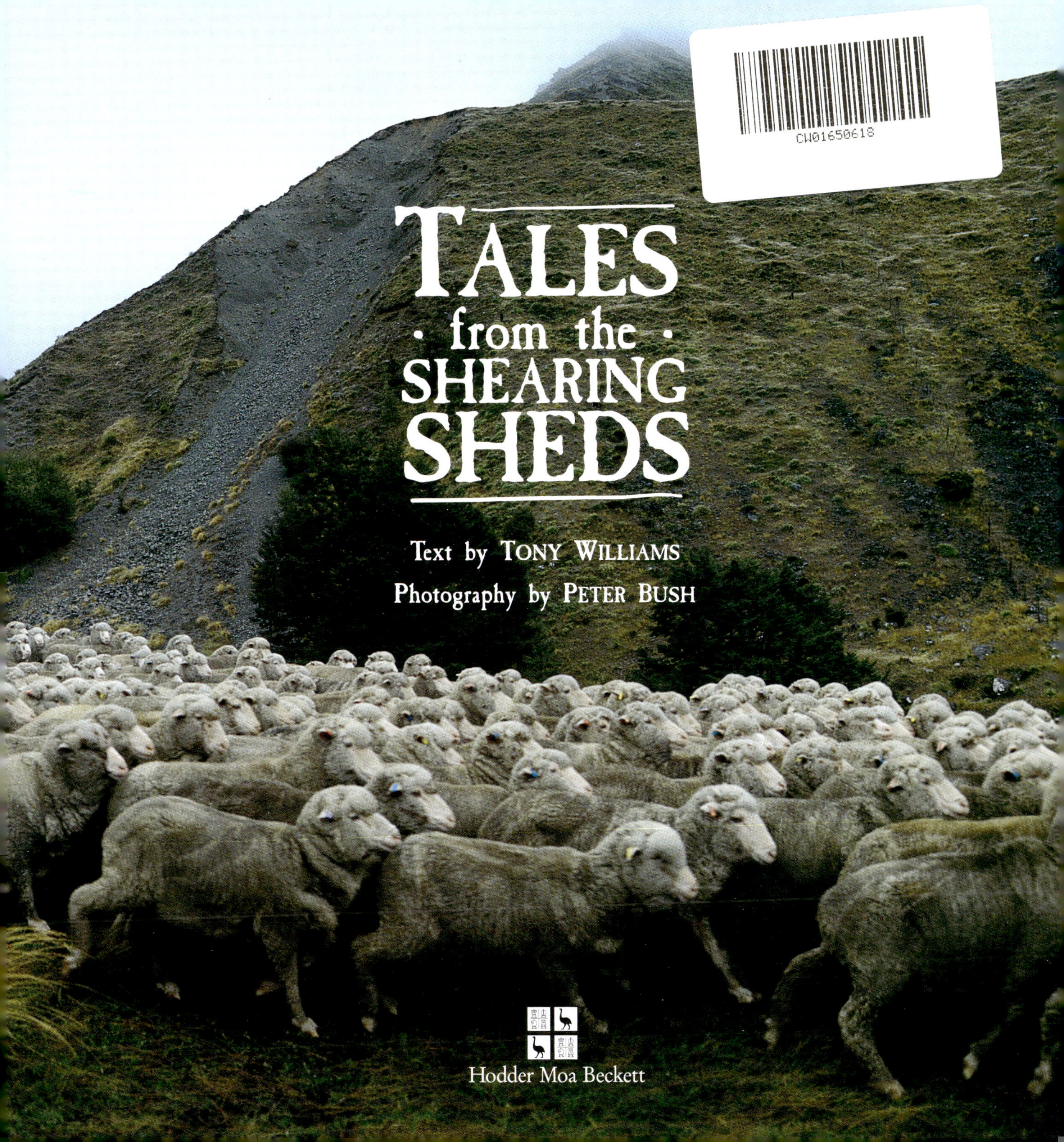

TALES · from the · SHEARING SHEDS

Text by TONY WILLIAMS

Photography by PETER BUSH

Hodder Moa Beckett

Tony Williams' Acknowledgements

The people I have to thank the most are the people from the shearing industry who talked to me, many of whom are mentioned by name in this book.

Additionally, I would like to thank Des Williams the editor of *Shearing* magazine, Shelagh Wilde the secretary of New Zealand Shearing Sports and Michelle Freebairn, secretary for the New Zealand National Shearing Championships. My thanks also to my typist Teresa Harvey and the staff at Hodder Moa Beckett. I would also like to thank my partner in crime Peter Bush, a fascinating travelling companion who is not short of a yarn or two himself. He also has a very succinct way of summing things up and I have to confess that one or two of the best lines in the book are his. During the course of our travels, Peter and I were also treated to abundant hospitality, both in the way of food and accommodation, from people in and associated with the shearing industry. But even more than that we appreciated the warmth and friendship with which we were treated. So it is a pleasure to be able to tell the story of a very hard working and sociable group of people. This is their tale and wherever possible I have let their words do the talking.

Peter Bush's Acknowledgements

Many thanks to all those great country folk who extended their wonderful hospitality to us and to the many people in the sheds who were so patient with me while I was photographing them.

In Memoriam

The authors and publishers would like to express their gratitude to Boss Hogg, Les Hokianga of Hokianga Shearing Contractors, who died earlier this year.

ISBN 1-86958-733-2

Published in 1999 by Hodder Moa Beckett Publishers Limited, [a member of the Hodder Headline Group]
4 Whetu Place, Mairangi Bay, Auckland, New Zealand

Designed and produced by Hodder Moa Beckett Publishers Limited
Printed by South China Printing, Hong Kong
Film: Microdot, Auckland

INTRODUCTION

If I wasn't a writer, then I would probably be a shearer. There is something appealing about the free-living, independent lifestyle of the shearing gangs. This colourful world is part of the Kiwi character, and one of the last rites of passage in rural New Zealand for people whose families have been shearing for generations as well as for "townies" who seek out a true test of their mettle.

With photographer Peter Bush, I travelled the backcountry roads – from Te Kuiti in the North Island to Otago in the South – to discover and capture the disappearing culture of New Zealand's shearing gangs. The lively tales and legendary characters we encountered along the way testify to the hard work, the passion, rivalry and humour of the sheds. Often the shearers and rousies speak for themselves and their words convey what Peter Bush has captured in his stunning photographs.

It is a back-breaking profession – there are easier ways to make a living but there is pride in a job well done. As the Piopio kid (Alan "Mickey" MacDonald) explained to me: "I've been shearing for 20 odd years. The first thing that attracted me to shearing is you got paid for what you did. Like, if you were working with someone and you both had a shovel and you were working harder than the other fellow on an hourly rate, you just got paid the same as him and I hated that, I've always attacked my work."

From down Wanganui way to the Greywacke of Canterbury and the deep deep South the people tell their stories and work on the stands. Many of them became friends and at journey's end my address book was bulging with new names. There are others of "no fixed abode" as they travel New Zealand and the world looking for the next job, the next pay. Come along on this journey to the New Zealand backcountry and enjoy the sights and sounds of a unique part of Kiwi culture.

Tony Williams

June 1999

Contents

Chapter 1 · WANGANUI

Down Wanganui Way

THE BALDY AND OSBORNE GANG

Where the tarseal ends, the real New Zealand begins. Just north of Wanganui we turned off the highway expecting to find our destination, a tin shearing shed, a kilometre or two down a gravel track.

Instead photographer Peter Bush and I found it 20 km along a no-exit road which wound through razorback hills that looked like ridged pyramids onto which the sheep seemed to cling as tightly as the green grass.

OPPOSITE PAGE: An old shearing shed at the end of a lichen covered fence.

BELOW: The Baldy and Osborne gang at Maewa Station.

Along the winding roads there are no signs to help us on our way and only a woman and a small child, wife and daughter of a shepherd no doubt, to point fingers where the roads forks, until finally we are alerted by the sound of bleating sheep. When we reach the next ridge we see buildings and cars, a long tin roof and next to it a hodgepodge of pens full of milling sheep, shorn or waiting to be shorn.

Where the gravel track peters out to grass is the 3440-hectare Maewa Station that Bob Payne has managed for the last 32 years. The owner of the local petrol station arched his eyebrows when Peter asked for directions. "Where are you from? Everybody knows where Bob Payne lives." At the end of the gravel track is where Bob Payne lives, with the odd bit of tarseal thrown down on the dangerous bends for frosty mornings. Apart from the stones thrown up under the wheels of the car, the only sound is silence and the occasional bleating of sheep. Along the way we pass an old shearing shed where the timbered walls are covered with lichen and the steps have bowed under the tread of many feet over the years. Nearby are abandoned shearing quarters, little more than a glorified hut with a brick hearth reaching towards the sky.

It has taken us about half an hour to make this trip along a road where

a tired driver could easily slide his car over the precipice to the 30-metre drop below.

It is a trip that Mere Osborne will make twice a day for three weeks while her gang are shearing at Maewa Station. At 3.30 am, when most townies are still snug in their beds dreaming about their Coco Pops for breakfast, Mere rises in darkness. She ensures her three-year-old daughter is still tucked up tight in bed and drives to the Maewa Station navigating by her headlights and the moon ready for a 4.40 am start.

She is the gang leader of the Baldy and Osborne gang. That is not their official title. They have no official title. There is not a lot of officialdom to be found in the shearing sheds. This is a world where individuality abounds.

They are the Baldy gang because the night before we arrived three of the shearers shaved their hair off (no, not with their shears!). They are the Osborne gang because most of them are related to each other.

ABOVE: Mere Osborne – poetry in motion.

"Dad works at a 20-stand shed in Perth. It's just awesome."
Donelle Osborne, rousie

Mere Osborne is a wool handler, the person who sorts the fleeces. Mere's schoolgirl daughter Cassie is a rousie (short for rouseabout), the person who gets the fleece from the shearer to the woolhandler. They are also known as shed hands, and in Australia are more grandly referred to as "wool fibre technicians." Cassie's cousin Donelle Osborne is another rousie. Danny Osborne is the ganger (lead shearer) and one of the shearers is 62-year-old Tommy Allan. He is also related to the Osbornes. So is his sister Lana, the gang's cook.

It's estimated there are about 40 Osbornes and their relations from the Wanganui region who are either still working in the shearing gangs or have done so in the past. One of them is a one-eyed Osborne who recently shore his first tally of 200 sheep in a day. The most famous of them is Glen Osborne, the All Black.

OPPOSITE PAGE: Smoko time – the discarded "moccies" awaiting the return of the shearers.

In any gang the leader is supposed to be the leading hand, but in the Baldy and Osborne gang the power definitely rests with Mere. She is a star who stands outside the spotlight and outside the public view but, like the great performer she is, she dominates the proceedings.

She is little more than medium height, with tight curly hair and eyes which are wide open and alert. She has the square shoulders of a shearer (though she has probably only ever shorn a sheep with her eyes) and stands with her back ramrod straight. On the back of her right shoulder, visible where her singlet pulls away, is the tattoo of a swallow.

She is a hive of energy, constantly moving and looking, swooping straight-backed to scoop the fleeces off the floor, jolting the gate to the shearing pens shut with a swift kick as she passes. She glides through the commotion of shearers and rousies with effortless balance.

This is a six-stand gang. A stand is simply where one shearer works. But it is more than that. It is his position and his status and his personal space. It is hallowed ground. While interviewing for this book I would never approach a shearer when he was shearing. When he was off the stand I would walk straight up to him, but when he was still on it, attending to his equipment or just sitting there smoking, I felt I could never intrude unless he invited me in with a smile, a word or a glance.

Sheds are described by how many stands they have in the same way cars are described by the number of cylinders they have. In the status of the shearing sheds a four-stand shed is normal, a five or six-stand is getting there and anything above that brings an eager smile to the face of a shearer or a rousie.

The shearing board is one of the best pieces of live theatre you will find anywhere. At the Maewa

BELOW: The Baldies are: (from left) Marshall Deaker, Cabbage (Bryce Kinloch) and Wayne Herring (with hair).

A Stitch in Time

I stitched up my mate's leg once when I was working in Dannevirke. He cut himself with a handpiece so we stitched him up. We used dental floss and a needle. He went to the doctor that night and the doctor told him he was mad. But he's still got his leg.

Cabbage (Bryce Kinloch), shearer

Pizzle Guards

We were in Australia out the back of Broken Hill and the contractor brought this new rousie out. This fella was a wee Aussie guy, he didn't know bugger all, he knew nothing, and he couldn't rousie for nothing. He was just useless. What they did, the boys got half a broom handle and tacked a bottle top on the end of it. They told him this was the pizzle guard for shearing wethers (castrated male sheep) and every time a shearer brought out a wether they'd yell out "pizzle guard" and this useless fella would come along and put this pizzle guard on the wether's dick and the shearer would shear around it. They had this guy doing it for two days.

Anon (one of the Baldy and Osborne gang)

Station, I watch entranced. There are six struggling sheep, six shearers with their backs bent, six right arms moving up and down, six metal handpieces swinging in motion, while the rousies move among the shearers with their brooms.

The brooms have plastic bases that slide across the timber floor, pushing the loose wool into piles. Originally the brooms had bristles, but these picked up straw and contaminated the wool.

The rousies are usually, but not exclusively, female. They are a cross between ballerinas and Mrs Mop, gliding the wool across the floor in elegant, circular motions. All of this is done to the raging beat of music blaring from a stereo turned up full. The beat monitors everything and many of the female rousies seem to dance as they walk.

To talk to another member of the gang above all this noise an ear needs to be leant towards a mouth, but no one shouts and they communicate more by motion than words. The rhythm of the music and the mutual motion of their work puts them into a type of harmony with each other where the raising of an eyebrow or a glance is often enough.

The motion of a shearing shed is both hypnotic and energising. After almost a whole day in this shed it became too much for me. I spotted an old cricket bat leaning against the shed wall and picked it up, starting to run through the repertoire of strokes of some imagined innings. Now I was contributing to the motion of the shed and so it began to contribute back to me.

"What you shear is what you get. If you don't work, you don't get paid."
Tommy Allan, shearer

ABOVE: The Man – Tommy Allan.

The presser Bruce Jones noticed what I was doing and picked up a knotted mass of wool off the floor and bowled it to me. I knocked it back at him. He bowled faster and this game continued with increasing velocity until it had to be abandoned when a fierce drive nearly removed Mere Osborne's head from her shoulders.

Along with the continuous motion there is a constant pressure in the sheds that some can't handle. The Baldy and Osborne gang started with two students this year. One couldn't hack it. The corridors of learning had not prepared her for the real world of sweat and hard work. She surrendered and returned to her classroom. The other, an art student called Rebecca who keeps her dreadlocked hair under a Rastafarian hat, was made of sterner stuff and she stayed.

Singlets are the uniform of the sheds. The shearers always wear them and the rousies usually do, though they sometimes prefer tattered old T-shirts. The more tattered the better. The rousies often have long hair and they tie it out of the way with a colourful bandanna or hairgrip, or they bundle it up under a hat. The shearers wear special shearing jeans which are double layered to prevent the grease from the wool penetrating them. On their feet they wear the traditional shearing moccy (moccasins) which these days are made out of leather or synthetic material. Years ago every shearer knew how to make them. Now they buy them.

The sheep are not particularly enthusiastic about being shorn. They mill around in pens on the other side of the gates. As the shearer passes through the gate he presses his tally counter, which is usually fastened to the gate post at about shoulder height. He grabs the nearest sheep under the front legs or around the neck and drags it back through the gate, sliding the sheep on its backside across the timbered floor to the stand where his handpiece is waiting.

The sheep is held tightly in this sitting position, its head wedged between the shearer's legs with the same unresisting reluctance of a long-haired lad getting an enforced haircut on the last day before he has to go back to school.

Black Humour

My Uncle Charlie was shearing out the back of Cal James' and he was shearing this black sheep and he said to one of his nieces, "Go up to my quarters and get my torch." She comes back with it and goes, "What's the matter uncle?" He said, "Oh just hold it on the sheep, I can't see it you know, it's too dark." And she did it… the boys were in fits.

Danny Tamehana, ganger

ABOVE: Danny Tamehana, ganger.

The sheep is shorn in a series of "blows" across specific parts of the body. First the belly is shorn, then the crutch, a hind leg, the neck and head, the shoulder and along the back (known as the long blow because here the shearer is able to make long sweeping strokes). Then the shearer comes down the "money side", the sheep's last unshorn side.

Finally, clad only in its underwear, the sheep is then pushed through the porthole of the stand and slides down the chute to where it will make its way back to the outside pens.

To do all this the shearer has to be part wrestler, part pool player and part barber. The wrestling is how he controls the sheep, using his arms and legs to move the sheep around. It is the sheep that must move, not the shearer, because the position of the handpiece is fixed at the end of a tube below the overhead motor or driveshaft.

The sheep has to be set up for each new blow in the same way in pool each shot must prepare the way for the next one. The sheep must get a really good, even haircut with no tufts of loose wool sticking up. A well-shorn sheep looks smooth and you can see the pink skin underneath.

A bad or novice shearer will often leave ridges of wool on the sheep so it looks like a lawn mown by a husband who'd rather have been fishing.

> "I just decided to do it until I knew what I wanted to do when I grew up and I'm still doing it."
> Marshall Deaker, shearer

If the shearer does the first two blows right the shearing is effortless. Some shearers are heavy on muscle, some on technique, but the real skill is in how they control the sheep. By the time they have finished, the sheep has been turned 180 degrees and is facing the porthole in such a way that with only a polite tap on the backside it will disappear down the chute. That's the theory. Often the sheep gets more of a shove. Occasionally the sheep ends up in the wrong position and makes a run for it, then it's an all-in wrestle to get it through the porthole.

The rousies pile the wool up for the wool handler who grades the wool, dragging out inferior or stained wool and throwing it into a separate heap known as the oddments pile.

The presser takes the quality pile, crams and tramps it into a bale. The wool is pressed tight into the bag which, when full, weighs about 180 kg and is about one cubic metre in volume.

The first time I ever saw a presser at work was when I went out to a shed where the cocky (the universally used slang for a farmer) was cutting costs by doing his own pressing. I am certain that he looked forward to the shearing gang arriving every year, the same way little kids wait for the white bearded man in the red suit.

OPPOSITE PAGE: Bruce Jones – the presser's job is all sweat and muscle.

BELOW: Keeping a tally.

This cocky was middle-aged but with short, cropped hair and biceps that could power the axle of a steam train. When he had crammed enough wool into the sack, he began working the crank with a steel lever as tall as he was. The lever was at an angle, so when he started it was above his head and he pushed it down to his waist, then up again, the resistance increasing at each push as the wool became more tightly compressed.

His muscles bulged as if they were going to pop out of his arms and the expression on his face was like that of a boxing champion I once saw watching a replay of one of his old fights. His teeth were gritted, his jaw jutting, his nostrils flared and there was real fire in his eyes. He was *loving* it.

These days some stations have hydraulic presses that will do the work for you. They cost about $15,000 and you can hear the sneer in a presser's voice when he tells you that. They use them, but it's not real pressing is it? If Arnold Schwarzenegger worked in the sheds, he'd definitely be a presser.

There's an absolute joy to pressing which I hope I can capture for you. It's the same strange pleasure you experienced as a child when you took some object, such as a cardboard box or a blob of clay, and tried to crush it down as small as it would go. It's the same thrill we get watching Batman or Indiana Jones nearly getting crushed by the walls of a shrinking room.

The Runny-Nosed Sheep

There was this new fellow and Russell Duncan who was pressing for us said to him, "There's a sheep in here with a snotty nose. Can you go and wipe it please, because we don't want to touch it." So he goes and gets an old shirt and blows its nose.

Danny Tamehana, ganger

As usual, despite the many family connections, the Baldy and Osborne gang came together casually and almost at the last minute, as contractor Lee Matson explained, "One went to America and said he's not coming back. Then a mate rang up from the South Island and he had a mate and he had a mate. One guy rang from America and said he was coming back."

Those who have been before often leave their mark on the side of the shed. This one was signed by "Hoppy 96 and 97" and "Kris 1995, 96, 97, 98."

The only thing you'll find shearing gangs have in common is there is little conformity. One member of the Baldy and Osborne gang was the distinguished sounding Bryce Kinloch, but Mr Kinloch is better known in the industry as Cabbage.

Cabbage was given the nickname because when he was a child he looked like a Cabbage Patch Kid, one of those little dolls with no hair and

Drunk Shearing

The fella I shear with at home, Archie, he doesn't drink at all now but what he used to do was unreal. One day old Archie got a crate of beer. By the end of the day the other shearers had to step over Archie 'cause he was sitting in the catching pen all day drinking beer and he wasn't going nowhere. One day they couldn't find Archie and they found him asleep in the horse trough.

Marshall Deaker, shearer

big ears. As a Baldy, Cabbage still has no hair and his ears could still flap on a windy day. He carries a bit of extra flesh for a shearer, but then Cabbage also has an extra glint in his eye that most don't.

Cabbage asked me to pass on a message to a contractor I was intending to visit. The message was a kiss for his wife. I was happy to oblige, but when I saw the contractor I wasn't so enthusiastic.

That contractor described Cabbage to me thus: "Cabbage is a cheeky bugger who can tell a lot of bullshit. He's a young fellow that went to school and didn't do any good.… so he decided to go out shearing. Shearing has helped to harden him up a bit. He actually looks like a damned good prop now… but he's useless."

All joking aside, Cabbage is actually a bit of a hero. Don't take my word for it, it's recorded on tape at Te Papa Museum; the tale of Cabbage, surgeon-general of the shearing sheds.

Tommy Allan is what Cabbage is still becoming – a legend in the shearing sheds. He was born in the Whanganui River district 62 years ago and has been shearing for about 46 years. "My dad had a run," he told me. "He had a shearing gang for years and I crashed [stayed] with him for a while and I started shearing and I never looked back. I just kept going."

Tommy had his own gang "for about 15 or 20 years" but gave that up to put his kids through school. When they graduated he went back to shearing. During the winter, he went out killing possums. He used to track them and poison them. When there was a bounty on possums, he was getting more money for killing possums than he was for shearing sheep. He used to sell the skins green and caught so many possums that he had to buy a freezer to store them in.

When asked how many sheep he has shorn throughout his working life, his answer is straightforward,

"I wouldn't have a clue. I did 340 or 350 most days when I was younger but now I've got to just plod on and take my time and make sure I don't break my body. I'll keep going till I can't do it.

"Now I'm the only shearer left in the Allan family up here anyway. My brother has shorn for me for years, but he's moved down south now. I've got a son shearing in Australia and that's the only one I've got shearing. All my other boys are not shearers at all. They have to choose their life I suppose.

"I'm always first up in the morning. I get up most mornings at three o' clock and put the jug on because it takes 25 minutes to boil. We've got a jug that holds 50 cups."

Apart from the early starts, Tommy is still pretty laid-back about life as this story by contractor Lee Matson shows.

"Last year Merv said to Tom, 'Do you want to come into town?' because Tom lived up the river a bit and he said, 'He can rent the little house I bought.' So Tom said, 'Yeah that'll be good.' So Tom rented the house and then he forgot to pay the rent and Merv rang me from America and said, 'Tom doesn't seem to be paying the rent,' so I said 'I'll sort it out.' I said to Tom 'Hey look you haven't been paying your rent', and he said, 'Oh no I haven't.' So now I take it out of his wages until he's caught up."

Family

We're all brothers and cousins so we're all family and we all stick together and people who come into my gang, they all know straight away if anything goes down. You're talking to everybody, not just that one person. So they never try and stir trouble. Most shearing gangs get on really well; it's like more of a family.

Danny Tamehana, ganger

Marshall Deaker was another member of the gang with the baldy haircut. He is from Waikouaiti, which is about half an hour north of Dunedin. He has left his wife and child down there to come north looking for work. It's November and this is mainshear for the North Island. Because of the different sheep and climate the shearing season varies in different regions of New Zealand. For that reason most shearers are itinerant, travelling to wherever the work is. Marshall has been shearing for 20 years and started when he was 18.

This is the first time he has worked in the North Island. It's a foreign country to him compared to Australia where he has shorn for about five years. The money was better over there, but his daughter

OPPOSITE PAGE: Bruce Jones throwing the wool into the air to blend it.

The Little Welshman

I said, "How many sheep can you shear?" and he said, "About 250." I said, "Oh well you'd better come on over." So anyway he turned up. He was only a little fella; he was 18 but he's a top little fella.

I've got a garage over Wanganui East. There's a room and a bed there so he camped in there and when it was time to go to work I said to him, "Come on we've got a job." So he arrived up there, set up all his gear, showed me all his gear – it looked a bit lumpy some of it – and then he started shearing. He'd shore about six sheep and I said to him, "Well son I think you'd better come with me; I'll book you into a shearing course with the New Zealand Wool Board." He can shear 250 sheep in a day in Wales because they've got hardly any wool on them. Anyone can shear 250 sheep in Wales.

Lee Matson,
shearing contractor

LEFT: Contractor, Lee Matson.

was five years old and due to go to school. He didn't want her speaking with an Australian accent so he headed home.

He came to shear for Lee Matson in Wanganui on the network that exists among shearers.

"A friend of mine I used to shear with in Aussie, he worked for Lee before, so I just talked to him and he said he was a good guy to work with, just to give him a ring, so I gave him a ring and here I am."

There is a saying in the shearing world that in any gang you go to there is always somebody who knows somebody you know. It's a brotherhood with more lines than the Mafia. If this country was ever invaded by a foreign power, it would be the shearers who would lead the resistance.

But forget the ganger, the wool classer, even the shearing contractor, everybody agrees the most important person in the gang is the cook. As an army marches on its stomach, so a gang shears on the quality of its tucker. Since the main fare is locally killed stock, the cook has to know 1001 ways to cook mutton.

The cook's "stand" is the kitchen. It's her personal fiefdom where she lays down the law. As we tucked into lunch at Maewa Station one of the shearers, Rob, looked up with surprise to find he had incurred the displeasure of the cook, Lana – better known as "Auntie." She rules the roost with a tongue that's not sharp but firm. She doesn't so much threaten as offer advice you'd better take.

Auntie Lana tells me she lives her life by three basic rules, "I don't smoke, I don't drink and I don't expect to pick up their rubbish."

That's where the unfortunate Rob strayed across the invisible line. In a court session lasting all of 10 seconds (from

ABOVE: Rob Pomare, still smiling despite his $1 fine.

RIGHT: Tommy Allan, and his sister Lana, the cook.

being charged to sentenced) she found him guilty of leaving a can on the table from breakfast and fined him $1.

She took his bemused caught-in-the-headlights look to be an appeal, so proceeded to show him the exact spot where the can had been left and added with slight threat this time, "and there was a mess underneath the table right there."

Rob quickly conceded the point.

Rule number one of the shearing sheds – don't mess with the cook.

A Shearer Who Made It

There's a fellow called Merv Henare and he's a real little character. He's a country boy who'd hardly even been to Wanganui when he came out and started working for us as a presser. Then he learned to shear and then just disappeared. The first time he went to Auckland is when he got on the plane and went to America. And then he went to England and he went everywhere. You couldn't see him now because he's all over the world. My garage in Wanganui East is sort of on an island. I've got the corner bit with the big workshop and garage and he owns the rest of the block almost. He's bought his mother a house and he's bought his sister a house. And he's got a place in Australia too!

Lee Matson, shearing contractor

Chapter 2 · EAST CAPE

East with The Vikings, The Mob and The Boss

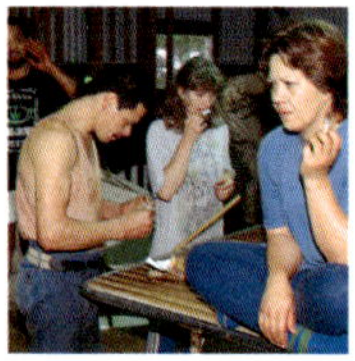

ABOVE: Michael Brown (left) and Meredith Dysart (centre), the leaders of the DB gang.

MOBS AND GANGS

On the East Coast of the North Island, a few kilometres south of Napier, is Ocean Beach. To get to it you turn off the main road, take a winding track and then pause at the top of a precipitous road which pitches down to where the blue Pacific Ocean caresses a golden, sandy beach.

A hill or two back from the ocean is the 1200-hectare Taurapa Station. As on most stations, the house is next to the road, but the shearing shed is tucked away out of sight. This time it is only 3 km away from the main highway along another road which is interrupted by eight farm gates. Each of them involves getting out of the car, opening the gate, driving through it and stopping the car to shut the gate again.

Halfway to the shed, the road dips down through a glade of leafy elm trees beside a stream. A brisk breeze whisks the tufts of toi toi fluff as if they were wisps of wool deposited by a passing wool truck.

Here the shearing shed has been built on two storeys with ramps for the sheep to get up to the shearing stands on the first floor. Unusually, the iron cladding on the walls is new. Usually shearing

LEFT: Boss Hogg (centre) and some of his shearing clan.

OPPOSITE PAGE: Shearers are professionals who maintain their tools with care.

sheds are covered as much with rust as with paint. Part of the floor has been re-timbered with chipboard and has less character than the closely boarded, older wood on the shearing board, which is stained tar black in places from the grease, sweat and dirt of the tens of thousands of sheep that have been shorn there.

We arrive during smoko to discover one of the rousies, Hine, knitting a jersey for her partner. The needles are huge, more like something you would use to stake seedling plants. But they are the right size for the wool, which is coarse and untreated. She collected it from the floor at another station and joins the strands by simply pressing them together. They hold – more or less. Hine is a bit of a trader and wants to swap a shearing T-shirt for a copy of this book when it comes out. She seems to believe her T-shirt has added value because she has already worn it.

"It goes back about 15 years. I used to hang out with my cousin. His name was Murray, but everybody called him Bob. Everywhere he was well I wasn't far behind or I was right there, so they used to call me Two Bob."

Tui Puna, rousie

BELOW:
A young Hokianga helping out in the shed.

Another rousie, Tui Puna, does not try to sell me the shirt off her back. She tells me her nickname is Two Bob. I ask why.

She tucks her hair out of the way under a pointed red and green hat that makes her look like one of Santa's helpers. A slightly elongated profile and a mischievous look in her eye add to the elfin appearance. She likes to play rugby league for the local Tangio club and has represented the Hawke's Bay league team for the last three years. As a concession to this, the day I met her she was wearing a rugby sock on one foot and a grey sock on the other.

She says she likes league because it is such a physical game and she enjoys the mental preparation required. Similar to shearing?

"Yeah, because you're moving all the time, especially when it comes to the main full wool. Fleece wool is quite physical. But league is sort of quite different because you've got that body contact. You don't have contact with the sheep, just the shearers, but when they get loose we've got to run after them and try and tackle them (the sheep, not the shearers) and put them back in their pens without dropping our broom, or that's a shout."

Like most people, Tui Two Bob entered the shearing industry through her father, starting out rousieing for him in 1982.

The presser Campbell has no shearing in his bloodline, but he has wide shoulders and strong arms and that's mainly what you need to handle the press. This one is a Sandow press, a type prevalent in the Hawke's Bay region. It's pretty basic and consists of two wooden crates, a pulley and a lever.

The wool is piled into one box, which has a bale in it, and into a second box, which has three long steel pins to stop the wool falling out. When both boxes are relatively full, the second box is winched on top of the first. The pins are removed from the top box and a winch presses the loose wool from the top box into the bottom box.

The top box is then taken away, any loose wool removed and the bale closed with hook pins. The front of the bottom box is then swung open so the bale can be pulled out and, with the help of a wooden-handled bale hook, is manipulated into the stack of other bales by the load-out door.

Today the gang are shearing lambs (not sweet, gambolling little lambs as a city dweller would imagine them, but sheep that are less than a year old). The wool comes off in tufts that are scraped with the brooms into a big pile, almost like a snowdrift. Campbell drops to his knees to embrace this pile of wool, then rises with a huge armload of it which he throws into the press.

By the end of the day there is a wet V on the back of his T-shirt, but a satisfied smile on his face. Four years ago he was unemployed, but local contractor Brendan Mahony "gave him a go." Some say Mahony is the biggest shearing contractor in New Zealand. As well as his Napier-based run; he also owns a share in a large run in the South Island. Many say he is also the cleverest contractor in New Zealand because he also owns a half share in the local pub. After he has paid his men he takes them down to his pub and gets his money back.

As I watched, a sheep was carried in by two of the station's shepherds and dumped on ganger Mike Edmonds' stand. It didn't get up and try to run away. It just lay there panting. The shepherds fetched it some water. I found out later that it had run into a steel fence and stunned itself. It was touch and go whether it would live, but at least they'd get the fleece off its back first.

If a sheep falls while waiting in the pen, with the other sheep squeezed tightly around, it will often suffocate. Later I saw one

The Good and the Hard Working

Our people they work so hard; they are decent honest people, the majority and yet it's very difficult to get ahead.

Mavis Mullins, shearing contractor

OPPOSITE PAGE: Backs bent, muscles flexed, handpieces whirring, and the fleeces fall away.

such sheep in a pen on another farm. The cocky, who was a big, stern-looking fellow, picked it up, held it at waist height and then dropped it. He did this several times and I almost expected the sheep to bounce. I assume he was trying to revive it, but he seemed more likely to finish it off.

That sheep from Taurapa Station on the East Coast didn't make it either. Later I found it lying outside. It was shorn and dying, the life slowly ebbing out of it. One question I have been asked by townies is, "Does shearing hurt the sheep?"

The Shearing Diet

There are some older guys who are coming back into the industry. They used to be shearers, went to the freezing works and found out they still live like a shearer. When you are a shearer you are burning so many calories that you can eat anything. If you eat a chop, you take the one with the most fat on it. When they stop shearing they still do that and the body can't take it and they get fat. So some of them are coming back into the industry to lose weight.

Koro Mullins, shearing contractor

The answer is I don't know because I have not yet found a sheep that could reply to the question. I am sure the shearing itself is painless, except for the odd careless nick of the shears, much like cutting yourself shaving. When the sheep goes down the chute it can look rough, but then again I know children who enjoy that sort of rough and tumble.

Townies can't really look at the rural industries from a townie viewpoint. I had a bit of a culture shock the first time I spent some time with a shearing contractor a few years ago. He was based in a one-horse town in the middle of the South Island that did not have a single set of traffic lights. The night I arrived this wild looking character knocked on the door of the contractor's house and asked him if he wanted to buy a wild pig for $200.

The next morning I encountered the pig lying dead on top of the garage freezer with its legs sticking up in the air. I went with the contractor when he tossed the skinned pig in the back of his station wagon and took it along to the local butcher (who worked from home not from a shop).

The butcher asked the contractor how he wanted it cut up. That was a new one on me, only ever having bought meat in packets. The

Shearing Joke

Q. In a shearing gang how can you tell the dogs from the men?

A. The men eat spuds with their meat.

butcher then took us over to his truck and opened the door to reveal a dead deer, hanging down from the ceiling rail which it was tied to by its legs. The deer's head lay on the floor of the truck with the huge, lifeless eye staring at me as I tried to put out of my mind thoughts of watching Bambi as an 8-year-old.

The throat of the deer had been cut and its trachea was hanging out like a length of hosepipe. You see, if you are squirming at this now it proves you are a townie. In the South Island rural community, you can forget your pastas and your vegetarian food. Here, meat is the staple of every meal. Townies eat it too, but someone has to kill it.

The Amateur Electrician

We've had the odd character staying in the quarters over the years. One old bloke was having trouble with the stove in the quarters. He reckoned he was an electrician and he got in there with a screwdriver and pliers and next thing bang, everything was blown.

Johnny Monson, cocky

Back on the four-stand board at Taurapa Station, shearers number one and four were men who were similar yet different. Neither was much taller than my shoulder. Ganger Mike Edmonds had a squat build, square jaw and deep-set eyes. His muscular body looked as if gravity was pulling it down towards the sheep. By contrast, Sam Tamati had a lithe muscularity. There was not a kilo of fat on his body and even his face was so sharp and angular you felt you could cut yourself on it.

Mike Edmonds paused from sharpening his cutter when I asked him how long he had been shearing. His calculations were interrupted by background shouts such as, "Be honest." Finally he came up with the answer.

"Twenty-seven years."

In that time he has turned his hand to other things, such as working in a freezing works, on a farm and erecting fences. So why did he come back to shearing?

"Because its better… better money. I tried a couple of town jobs there and it's not the same. [In the sheds] people are always friendly, you can

BELOW: Ganger Mike Edmonds.

sit down after work and have a few beers and a chat. There's too many people in town and they all want to do their own thing, like head off home after work. I wasn't really into that sort of thing."

I inquired about a raw-looking red mark Mike had on his arm.

"It's a hoof, it kicked back. Sometimes they get a bit stroppy. I'm too tired to fight them now," he added with a wry smile.

Sam Tamati had a very different style of shearing from Mike Edmonds'. In fact, no two shearers ever shear the same way. Though the sheep may seem the same and the blows may be struck the same way, each has his own signature style, as individual as fingerprints. Sam's style was easy and economical.

He had been shearing for 12 years. He lived on the outskirts of Napier and was married with four daughters. That's why he works so hard, so he can afford the dowries to marry them off one day!

Sam comes from a shearing family. He was one of four brothers who were all shearers, but he is the only one still shearing.

One now works in a diamond mine in Australia, while the other two left shearing gangs to join two other quite different types of "gangs." One works for Social Welfare and the other is the president of the Napier Mongrel Mob. He lives in a fortified house because "he has to." If only he had stuck to shearing.

Where the Hogg Is King

We travelled inland from the coast to find Boss Hogg, who is a legend in Hawke's Bay. When others describe Boss Hogg they simply say, "He is as wide as he is tall" and "He is two-thirds of an All Black front row." He does not shear anymore, but instead has been known to run his gang from an armchair placed in the shearing shed where he can watch his shearers sweat.

LEFT: Another sheep heads for the chute.

Feast Time!

Two very poetically named members of the Hokianga clan are Taranaki (Naki for short) and Hawke's Bay Hokianga. It reached a stage where both of them were so fat from their love of food they decided they must do something about it. They admitted themselves to hospital where they had their mouths wired shut so they could only drink fluids and not partake of all the rich and fattening food that tempted them so. When they came out of hospital, the family were so delighted to have them back they threw a huge party in their honour. When Naki and Hawkie saw all that food laid out they went and got the pliers, pulled the wire out of their mouths and tucked into the feast with the rest of the family.

Anon

His real name is Les Hokianga and the company goes by the name Hokianga Shearing Contractors, but are more generally known as Boss Hogg's Termites.

That story about his weight isn't a myth either. When the All Black Incomparables won a series in South Africa for the first time in 1996, the prop Olo Brown weighed in at 105 kg, and the hooker Sean Fitzpatrick at 106 kg. That makes a total weight of 211 kg, which was Boss Hogg's top weight – so he really could have been two-thirds of an All Black front row.

"As you can see, I'm quite a big guy," he told me, settled into his armchair as comfortably as a bird nesting on an egg. "I never used to be this big. I used to be about 15 stone. I was a shearer myself. I've shorn over 400 lambs in a day. Now I weigh 180 kg. When I gave up shearing, when I was 26, I came back to Hastings and I ended up in the freezing works. I used to start at five in the morning and finish at 10 and I used to go straight from there to the pub every day and get pissed. And that's where I started putting the weight on. I used to play senior A rugby. Started off as a five eighth and ended up as a hooker. I was pretty mobile then. I'm not too hot now."

Boss Hogg has passed both his real name and his nickname, as well as some of his mana, on to his eldest son Les Hokianga, the lead ganger. Les junior is often known as Little Boss which gives Les junior's wife Stella the right to go by the name Little Lady Boss.

You pretty much have to be part of the family to work for Hokianga Shearing Contractors. The business was started 62 years ago by Boss Hogg's grandfather and is being carried on today by Les senior. Boss Hogg's grandson, 10-year-old Tawa, assured me as he sat in his grandfather's ample lap, that one day he too is going to be a shearer and carry on the tradition.

There is a real family atmosphere in the shed with the continuous circular motions of the rousies being complemented by the similar ever-diminishing circles being run by the younger Hokiangas – Teren (five), Ezra (four), Ivan (two), and the baby rousie of the team, Charmaine (one).

It's always been like that with the Hokianga family Boss Hogg told me.

"About 15 or 16 years ago, when my father was contracting, we had 12 shearers, two pressers, 16 workers and 21 kids in the shed and my mother cooked for both lots and she was hard out all day, poor old Mum. She used to feed the kids first and then all the workers after. And when the kids used to come back from school, she used to give all the kids tea and then all the workers tea."

According to local folklore, all the Hokiangas are about five foot one inches tall, but they are also very good at sports and many Hokianga names are on the rolls of honour of sports teams in Hawke's Bay. It is also part of the legend that they love their tucker. The tale about Taranaki and Hawke's Bay Hokianga was told to me hundreds of kilometres away in the middle of the South Island. I don't know if it's true and, even if it isn't, it still represents the ebullient spirit of the Hokiangas and illustrates how their legend has reached the far corners of New Zealand.

The Co-op Gang

Through a green gate and down another winding gravel track, tucked behind a cluster of trees, in lightly falling rain, we found the shearing shed of cocky Max Butcher on his Karapiti Farm. Behind the shearing shed was a good, old-fashioned, long drop dunny with no chain to pull, no soap, and no mirror in which to straighten your tie.

Max runs the farm with his wife Ranee. Ranee wasn't shy in coming forward and giving the sheep short shrift if they were shy about coming forward to be shorn.

The sheep were Romney crossbreds and their rich, luxuriant fleeces came off in long white carpets. When tossed onto the table, the air caught underneath each of the fleeces so they floated down like billowing silk. As soon as the fleeces lay flat on the slatted wood a many-handed beast descended upon them, plucking out the oddments.

BELOW:
The Co-op gang.

That action is much like a harp player plucking at the strings, and though no sound is made, the physical beauty and grace of the action is similar.

The official name of the Co-op gang is the DB Omahu Open Shearing Gang. They share the hard work and the profits. Though none of them look in the least like any of the others, they all claim to be related to each other. The DB does not stand for the well-known beer of the same name but Dysart/Brown, the two leaders of the gang.

Meredith Dysart is a skinny, long-haired Pakeha female and Michael Brown is a tautly muscled Maori ganger. They are neither related nor married, their union is a lot more intimate that that.

This is a three-stand gang. As with any gang, the lead ganger is number one and down it goes in order of speed. Number three is John Kokiri.

He ties a white bandanna around his grey hair. As he pushes the sheep through the chute and straightens his back, he seems a little weary. Yet his walk is a saunter of pride, for there is nobility in work and each sheep he has shorn adds to his pride and his mana.

Next to him on number two is Rewa Mason, beefy and well built, his whole left forearm is graffitied by the fading blue ink of tattoos. His clothes have holes in them, they are not made for the job and neither yet is he. There is a scowl on his face; each sheep is a day's labour, hard physical work done for money not mana. When a sheep backs away from the chute and makes a run for it, he grabs it and wrestles it back into the porthole with brute force.

The best shearers are in harmony with the sheep, but Rewa is opposing them. When he lets another sheep escape from the pen, one of the rousies, Taini, grabs it by the scruff of the neck and holds it with legs astride until Rewa comes out of the gate to grab it.

ABOVE: Presser, Victor Hepi.

RIGHT: Victor Hepi and Ranee Butcher.

At number one is Michael Brown, a mix of the other two shearers. Like Kokiri he has a moustache, but his hair is black and caught in a ponytail. He has the same lithe body as Kokiri and he has a feel for the sheep, but he is younger and fitter. He has the same strength as Rewa Mason, but he uses it in harmony with the sheep and that's why he is the number one.

Ass Kickin'

ABOVE AND BELOW: Contractor Koro Mullins.

On the Viking Trail

From the 9th to the 11th centuries AD the Vikings swept across Europe in their longboats, armed with double-edged axes and a wild spirit that knew no fear. These fierce invaders went as far east as Greece. Westwards they colonised Iceland and Greenland. A full five centuries before Columbus stumbled onto America, the great Viking leader Leif Ericson found a coast that was "well wooded and with low hills." He had discovered America first. And onwards the Viking marauders sailed until finally they arrived in New Zealand.

Well not quite. They arrived a full seven centuries later and in sailing boats not longboats. They came as immigrants not raiders and a good many of them settled in the Dannevirke area, east of Hawke's Bay. There the chief, as far as shearing contracting goes, is Koro Mullins.

His territory ("run" in shearing contractors' language) extends intermittently from Dannevirke as far north as the famous Lochinvar Station near Te Kuiti. At the height of the season he employs nine gangs comprising 38 shearers and 38 associated staff. On a good day his crews will shear about 7000 to 8000 sheep.

Koro's ancestry does not extend from a raping and pillaging Viking, but from the Irish on one side and the Maori on the other. The Irish side would explain his gift of the gab; one of his ancestors must have kissed the Blarney stone. He commentates in many of the big shearing shows and as one middle-aged male wool handler said about him, "That Koro is a cheeky bugger. It doesn't take him two seconds to take the mickey out of anybody."

The Maori side would explain the mana that just glows out of him. He's the sort of person you immediately trust, the sort that you could turn up to shear for, ask him to put your previous pay (in cash) somewhere safe, and then not even bother to count it when he gave it back to you.

His Viking queen is Mavis Mullins. She has that classic beauty that grows from the inside out and lingers even when her children are passing into adulthood.

Many Maori carry the traditions of the past with them and so it is with Koro and Mavis. The benefit of the previous generations flows through them.

Their run was originally founded by Lui Paewai who is still the youngest

Not Service, Just Doing Your Job

We were talking to these quality auditors about how our people worked and I explained one instance where one of our customers, a farmer, needed to have sheep shorn and on a boat at 10 am one morning. And he told us the afternoon before!

That meant our people having to leave Dannevirke at 2 am, to get there at 5 am to do four hours' work to ensure that the sheep were on the truck ready to go. The quality auditors could not believe that our people would make that type of effort. In rationalising it out to them we just had to explain that as far as our people are concerned this industry is their industry. We might be the contractor, but we are nothing without them and we all recognise that we are all doing this together and it is a team job.

Mavis Mullins, shearing contractor

player to have played for the All Blacks. He was a Dannevirke man through and through, having been born there on 10 August 1906, and still there 64 years later on 2 January 1970, when he departed this life.

As a young man he was educated at Maori Agricultural College and played most of his rugby at five eighth. He was described as, "… unorthodox in his methods; he is difficult to anticipate and quick off the mark."

He made his first-class debut just nine days after his 16th birthday and was selected to play for the All Blacks just 45 days after his 17th birthday. He toured with the 1924 Invincibles and played a total of eight matches for New Zealand.

That rugby tradition is continued today by his descendants Nathan and Murdoch Mullins, who played for the Central Vikings rugby team.

Koro and Mavis see their ownership of the run as a trust for the future.

"My grandfather owned the run in the 50s," Mavis explained. "And then my father and his four brothers bought the run off him. They used to use the shearing to buy their own farms and once that all happened, we were just starting to become a part of the whole industry and Koro and I bought the run in 1989."

"When did I start? I don't remember a start and I can't even see a finish either, because we have family now who are very involved. Our children, we assume, will be involved. It's that Maori thing, we are just caretakers for this business. Maybe our children, maybe others in our industry. When people come to work for us they virtually become a part of our family. If there are people working for us now who show

> "I was brought up in the sheds. When my father was shearing I was a kid that used to go with him on campouts. A lot of our clients which we have today, I used to play tag in the woolsheds with."
>
> Mavis Mullins, shearing contractor

the potential and the inclination, we are quite happy to take them on and take them further if that is what their wish is."

In their business, Koro and Mavis have brought together their Maori heritage and a mix of the modern, electronic, business world. But Mavis' father, whom they bought the run from, shakes his head at the sort of things that go on today.

"He used to pay the wages once a year," Koro told me. "Though the shearers were entitled to an 'advance' on their wages. He only paid tax once a year. Now the Government wants to collect its taxes every fortnight."

"The cockies are still used to paying once a year," Koro says. "It's quite tough. In those days there was no such thing as an overdraft facility, but these days we have to have them. Nowadays, when I tell Mavis' father what we go through he thinks we are mad having to do what we are doing."

Paewai Mullins Shearing were the first shearing contractors in the world to be accredited ISO 9002. The second was a contractor in Australia and the third, Jim Malcolm of Ohai, just happens to be one of Koro's relations.

BELOW: Koro's office is filled with pictures of his company's shearing past stretching back to Lui Paewai.

The ISO 9002 inspectors had found nothing to prepare them for the level of "service" that is provided in the industry, though no shearer or rousie would ever use that word. They think of it as just doing their job. They don't have to go to any fancy college to be taught it. It's ingrained and natural.

"Unfortunately, the way the industry is going, you have to have so many business skills to be able to survive," said Koro.

"Contracting is a tough sort of a job,"

Mavis agreed. "You're the meat in the sandwich all the time. It's the sort of thing you can do to the nth degree. There's real burn-out."

Not that Koro and Mavis will get burned out. When it's time to turn over the run to the next generation (that's when Koro's got white hair – if he's got any hair left then at all – and Mavis looks matronly and spends all her days at the spinning wheel), their heritage will no doubt be passed on to the next generation in good condition.

The Perfect Quarters

The farmers used to supply the quarters, but now they are a bit pinched and they are letting those places go. It's not the Ritz but as long as there is plenty of hot water, a good mattress and a good cook everybody is content.

Koro Mullins, shearing contractor

Changing Times

The gangs used to live in the quarters on the job, but they don't now. In those days it was five o'clock starts, five runs instead of four. It was a long day. You'd have to start the shed, you'd have to kill the mutton for them, supply the mutton for them; it's a whole different ball game today in respect that they all go home to their wives, families, the pub, the TAB and everything else connected with it.

Johnny Monson, cocky

Chapter 3 · CANTERBURY

Into the Greywacke of Canterbury

ABOVE: Dean Cox, shearer, and son of shearing contractor, Adrian Cox.

INTO THE GREYWACKE OF CANTERBURY

After Christmas we headed south to catch the mainshear in the South Island, though even that can vary from region to region.

We crossed the raging seas (Cook Strait ferry in a squall) and landed on the Mainland of New Zealand about which American travel guides never fail to mention the fact that it is all covered by just one dialling code.

When you have lived in or passed through the great metropolises of London, New York and Los Angeles, the South Island seems almost uninhabited by comparison. But you also get the feeling that this peace and serenity is what the rest of the world should have. There are few places you get that feeling more strongly than in Pleasant Point, South Canterbury. About 20 km east of Timaru, the road sign boldly announces, "Pleasant Point – The name says it all."

OPPOSITE PAGE: Jim Morris' spectacular high country farm

It is the type of town where the school bus is the old-fashioned type with rounded wheel arches. It looks like it could have taken two (or three) generations of local children to and from school. Out here they don't let old machines die with indignity – they maintain them with dignity. On the main street is a taxidermist with a grizzly bear in his shop. Around here even the animals are maintained – they get stuffed.

BELOW: Deer culling at Morven Hills Station.

A group of workers eat their lunch sitting in the shade of a Trading Store. A shopper walks by and passes the time of day with them – everybody knows everybody else around here.

But they don't know me. Later I found out from Adrian Cox, the local shearing contractor, that they forgot to stamp my passport with the designation of JAAFA when I arrived on the Mainland.

I claimed ignorance, so he explained. "Just Another Arsehole From Auckland."

But before I discovered that I had to find him. His partner Lana gave directions over the phone in the clipped, no-nonsense manner of country folk.

"Down a dirt track, two-storey brown house with a white van and a heap of cars outside."

First she had to ask me my location, but even a JAAFA can work that out when he is standing in the main street of a one-horse town.

When we found her house, I saw that she had not mentioned that it was opposite a steep bank that rose all the way up to the horizon. On top of it a horse stood accentuated against a blue sky. It looked as if the horse was standing at the end of the world. The striking thing about the South Island is not just the serenity of the blue lakes, the jagged splendour of the mountains, or the treeless plains that seem to reflect your own thoughts back at you. The striking thing is that there is beauty almost everywhere you look.

Take the rusting old drum, which we encountered after Adrian and Lana had given us more directions to another shearing shed. We came across it on the road to Geraldine, along long, straight roads aimed at a mountain peak framed by trees on one side and a hedge on the other. I noticed that in the country the trees seem alive, not ignored as in the city. And here they provide more than decoration, they protect against the wind on a cold day and the sun on a hot one.

The drum was sitting on the other side of the fence at a rest area we stopped at. In the city, rust is a disease and rusty objects are thrown out in the annual hard rubbish collection. Here it signifies something that has nobly fulfilled its working life and is slowly being consumed by the environment.

Our tea finished, we moved on in search of the next shed. We found it eventually after making a wayward trip up the gravel track towards Mesopotamia Station. Peter had been there a couple of decades before with snow chains on the wheels of his car to photograph the station in the depths of winter.

But there was no snow on the ground today, just dust, and when we had gone too far along the dirt track we knew we had missed our turning. We were certain of this because this time our no-nonsense directions had included the words, "the tarmac goes right up to the shearing shed."

We turned back and found Otematata, one of the biggest Merino properties in New Zealand, nestled on a plain surrounded by the distant mountain peaks, the High Claytons, Hewson, Ben McLeod and the Four Peaks Range. Past the station and out of sight, unless you are on the high

ground, is the Rangitata River. On my old AA map, which was reclaimed from a garage sale and which tells the distances in miles, a ferry is marked nearby, but it is doubtful that it is still there today.

It was an idyllic, hot summer's day. We looked down at the pastoral scene below, standing beside thistles that were visited by butterflies and bees as the wind plucked the down from the heads of the thistles and gently blew it in through the open windows of the car.

Whereas in the city sound is something that assaults you, in the country it seduces you: the revving of a farm bike, the clattering of a truck being unloaded in a tin shed about half a kilometre distant – but sounding like it is right in your ear – the distant bleating of sheep. All these sound friendly and near.

Inside the shearing shed at the Otematata Station, the gang shears on an elevated stand 1.2 metres wide and 1 metre high. This makes it easier to keep the shearing and wool sorting area separate. The rousies reach across at shoulder height and pick up the fleece off the board with their hands or scrape it clean with a flat board.

ABOVE: The gang at Otematata, intrigued by a book about Australian shearers.

There is an old clock on the wall, but no one keeps time by it. The beat is the clack clack of brooms, the banging of the gates and the cutters razoring back and forth. Here the music is not as loud as the sound of the shearing, and the roar of the handpiece makes it sound like heavy metal.

This is a six-stand gang with only four rousies. One of them is Jasmine, the daughter of Lana. Jasmine wears an Adrian Cox Shearing Contractors T-shirt, runs barefoot through the wool and holds her hair back with a gold metal hair band. She also drives a car which has a registration plate which reads YRUNOC.

My guess was she had bought the car for her boyfriend to borrow and the registration was intended to read as, "YR [you're a] UNOC [eunuch]."

Apparently innocent, Jasmine didn't even know what a eunuch was and instead I discovered the number plate was meant to read, "Y [why] R [are] U [you] NOC [nosy]?"

As in most sheds, these are vibrant female rousies. I try to interview one who wears her hair in a ponytail and a wide, red bandanna with white stars on it that almost covers her forehead. But she gives

OPPOSITE PAGE: John Walls' bungee eases the strain on his lower back.

her name only as "Umm". Whether this was from shyness, because she was on the run from the police, or she was actually giving me her personalised numberplate, I was never able to discover.

The shearers were more forthcoming. Tony "The Tiger" Beck has been shearing for eight years. Tony is young, strong and probably a pin-up on some rousie's wall. On his left bicep is an Indian Brave in a warlike pose. On his back is a tiger – the tail curling out from under his singlet onto his right shoulder. Like many shearers, there is a touch of wildness about him. He has a dash of mischief in his eyes and a well-pitched, dry sense of humour which quickly becomes evident.

"You don't find many Australians out there. They're too lazy. They don't like getting out of bed and the sheep are too tough for them."

Tony Beck, shearer

"My grandfather used to be a shearer. My father is just an old freezing worker. He took the soft option. I skipped a generation, though shearing has been in the family a while. My uncle is a contractor in Aussie. I have been over there four times. It's all right if you can put up with Aussies. You are mostly working with Kiwis anyway.

"There's some pretty rugged places over there, shearing-wise. Sometimes you struggle to shear 100 sheep. They're wrinkly, with big dewlaps and heaps of wool on them. If you cut the neck you could kill them and you feel like doing it sometimes.

"You could be shearing about 600 km away from town. Quite often you come out of the quarters and you come across a snake or something like that that's minding it's own business. It normally ends up dead. You whack it with sticks or stones."

A couple of stands along, John Walls shears with the benefit of a harness which hangs from a rope tied on an overhead beam. Three giant springs come down to a curved bar with padding on which he rests his torso as he leans forward to shear the sheep. He calls it his "bungee".

In Australia there were a couple of Maori fellows, and one night they ran into the back of the pub in a car. They had had a few to drink. They didn't get into any trouble. The publican was a pretty good fellow.

John Walls, shearer

He began using it about five years ago when he experienced difficulties with his back. Some shearers do, after many years of bending over the sheep to shear them, though the shearing position is actually not as uncomfortable as it looks. It all depends on technique and discipline. The technique is to keep the spine straight, so there is no pressure on any individual vertebra. Most shearers are educated about this now and many of them walk around with their backs ramrod straight like guardsmen.

After each shear, the shearer straightens and fetches the next sheep from the pen. They usually do this in a strange, almost crab-like shuffle, deliberately pushing out the hips to leave a hollow in the small of the back. It is halfway between the correct standing and bending postures, as if coming up too quickly will give them the "bends" like a diver.

From this position the shearer leans forward and catches the next sheep in the pen. At that point the back snaps vertical again. He drags the sheep out, then leans forward, straight-backed, to pull the cord to restart the machine, picks up his handpiece and he's off again.

The discipline for shearers is to maintain the correct posture even when they are getting tired. Correct posture alleviates back problems. However, since he has been using the harness, John Walls has found his shearing has sped up. When I suggest that maybe many more shearers could use a bungee to improve their tallies, whether they have a bad back or not, we both laugh spontaneously. We know it will never happen. Even if the harness could increase tallies, it just doesn't fit in with the macho image of the shearing sheds.

The presser in this gang, Willie Sharp, is a world champion. He won the world championship in 1996. He has the aura of a champion about him. He is strongly built, but not muscle-bound. He stands with his shoulders thrown back and his chin held high as if he's sizing you up. But not in an unfriendly way. He is quietly spoken and he reminds me of the great All Black Michael Jones. Beneath the quiet veneer is a person of great depth. Like Michael Jones, he doesn't do much talking; he just retains his focus and lets his deeds do the talking for him – the true mark of a champion.

That's why Willie is the only person to have won the Golden Shears Pressing Championship three years in a row from 1994 to 1996, and to have been a woolpressing pairs champion four times. He says he intends to win the next world title in the year 2000 as well.

Recently he has taken the soft option and moved to the South Island where they have more sheep and use the easier hydraulic presses. But life isn't that easy, there's still the bane of a presser's life to put up with – the shearers.

They like to take the pins out of the press when the presser has his back turned, so when he presses the wool, the sides fall out. Another trick they like to play is to unplug the electrical cord and hide it.

In revenge, the pressers will nail the shearers' moccies (moccasins) to the floor, and laugh when they don't realise it until they step into them and try to walk away. Willie describes being in the shearing gang as like "a big happy family".

World champions aside, the "man" of this gang is undoubtedly Bruce Hopa. He is small and wiry, no longer a spring chicken, but not destined for the oven yet either. He moves with the intense energy and concentration of a man half his age. When he gets hot (which usually happens about a dozen sheep after smoko) he takes his singlet off and shears bare chested. When he shears, his head is lower than anyone else's, his eyes closer to the sheep. Sometimes there is a cigarette between his lips, the lighted end almost close enough to singe the wool.

According to the hecklers in the shed, he started shearing before the First World War. He laughs and gives his own version, "Since I was in short pants mate." Then he casts his mind back further. "I can remember my grandfather getting off the Tainui canoe with a couple of sheep and he told me to crutch them."

When the laughter has subsided he gets more specific. "I was raised on a farm in the Waikato. I started shearing in about 1957, but did not take it up full time until 1960. There were no shearing schools back then. I had to learn by watching the other shearers. In the lunch hour I'd get a brush, make out it was a handpiece and copy the blows like how they do on the sheep."

Irish Eyes Aren't Smiling

At Fairton, three miles north of Ashburton, lives the Thomas family who bring their daughters up strong and independent. When one of them was in Ireland, she offered to put her name down for a local shearing contest. All the Irishmen laughed at her. They weren't laughing when she came second.

Ex-husband of one of the daughters

He moved down to Timaru in 1967. "I like it around here, lots of shearing around here. It keeps you going all year round."

Bruce has a twinkle in his eye and a sense of mischief about him. Just before we arrived, the gang was playing a game of passing messages down the line. The rousies were telling Bruce to slow down because he was going too fast.

Bruce sent a message back down the line, "That's good because when I die I'll have written on my tombstone, 'He died doing hard work.'"

Bruce has a relationship with the sheep he shears. He talks to them as if he is married to them, and with his deep, throaty voice tells them to "Get that bloody leg up." His hair is slowly turning grey – one grey hair for every sheep he's shorn. He will still be shearing when his hair turns white, maybe when he has no teeth at all.

Picture the scene when the day finally comes when Bruce has shorn his last sheep and the stonemason gets the chance to chisel the words on his tombstone, "He died working *bloody* hard." Bruce is dressed in his woollen overcoat and is ready to go off to that great big shearing shed in the sky. Just as all the tearful relatives are standing around the coffin wailing and weeping, they suddenly freeze with shock as, from inside the coffin, there comes an almighty bang and they hear Bruce's unmistakable voice bark out, "Eh, get that bloody leg up".

Land of the Blade Shearer

From South Canterbury we headed further south through picture postcard countryside, skirting Lake Tekapo where the water was as fresh and clear as the first water that fell from the skies. In the distance a cloud spanned two mountain peaks, forming a bridge that will never feel the tread of feet.

We paused before a monument that was erected in celebration of the collie dog by runholders in the Mackenzie Country, then drove along the long, straight road that crosses the plains where James McKenzie drove his sheep over a century before. He was the biggest shearer of them all. Not only did he take the fleeces, but he took the sheep as well. In time he has become a folk hero.

His modern counterpart as a folk hero, though for shearing sheep not stealing them, is generally and affectionately known as Munga, but when he puts his name down for shearing competitions, the officials print Barry Taylor on the forms.

BELOW: Champion blade shearer Peter Casserly.

It was at the Omarama Hotel that I first had an inkling of the legend of Munga. It was not just what people said about him, it was the way they said it. There was an edge of awe and respect in their voice as if to say, "Oh you've really got to meet this character."

If you don't know where Omarama is, it is due east of Oamaru in the middle of blade shearing country. The Omarama Hotel is slap-bang in the middle of Omarama. Omarama is a one-horse town, so if you are in the main street and can't see the hotel, it means you're in the wrong one-horse town.

The Omarama Hotel lays claim to being the horniest bar in New Zealand. That's what it says on a sign under a stuffed stag in the bar. Little did I suspect when we checked into the hotel that the owner, Peter Casserly, was himself a former blade shearer and contractor. You can't go very far in the South Island without bumping into a shearer somewhere along the line.

The hotel was full when we arrived, but they still had two beds spare. It was a twisted walk through the kitchen, squeezing past the kitchen staff out through the back to a courtyard where there were two huts. Beyond them in the backyard, a magpie hooked its beak at a piece of meat thrown out for the dog.

Over the door of our room was a sign which said "Drinking Court". When Peter was contract shearing it used to be used as shearing quarters. Now they use it for anyone who is too drunk to drive home. Or for any vagrant writers and photographers who happen along.

Peter Casserly won the Omarama Merino blade shearing title aged 47 (he was nearly 48) in 1995. He was egged on by accusations he should have retired long before. He was the New Zealand blade shearing champion in 1975 and 1976, and the world champion in 1980. In 1976, when he was a *mere* 28 years old, he set a world blade shearing record when he shore 353 Perendale lambs in a working day. In shearing, world record attempts are pre-planned and have proper officials in attendance to accredit the tallies and check the quality of the shearing.

In blade shearing, the shears are like giant scissors. They are spring loaded so that the shearer's hand muscles do not cramp from constant squeezing and releasing. The blades are so sharp that each "blow" actually cuts in a sweep.

Blade shearing is slower than using a handpiece (usually up to 250 sheep are shorn in a day), but it leaves more wool on the sheep, without which they would die when the cold weather hits the high country of the South Island.

There are no stands in blade shearing because the shearers do not need to be hooked up to electricity. Often they will shear in a huge circle with the sheepos bringing the sheep to them and removing the wool. The only reason electricity is needed is for the radio which, in the lore of blade shearers, "is the noisiest thing in the shed."

The high country has bred some tough characters over the years. One is Jim Hura. His catch phrase used to be, "I'll see yer right, I'll see yer right, but you won't see mine." He was an 114 kg Maori who served in three wars, the Second World War, Korea and Vietnam. At night he used to enjoy telling tall tales, such as the one about killing Germans in the Second World War and eating them at hangis.

"He used to smoke eels," Peter said. "The kids loved him.When my kids were little they would all be around the campfire at night with him eating all the eels. Eels the size of a cup. He used to dry them for two or three days in the wind, taking them in at night, and take the backbone out and then put pepper and salt on them and grill them with chutney."

Unfortunately, Hura committed the ultimate crime in the shearing shed, a crime far worse than murder. He once punched the (male) cook because there were lumps in the gravy.

But tales of the mighty Munga fascinated me most of all. A man as big as a doorway with a personality twice that size.

I heard the tale about Munga and the Aussie ram from several sources. It is now part of the folklore of the shearing sheds. Then there was a tale, just a few months before, of Munga winning the Alexandra show. He had bought a sheep-dip business and been out of competitive shearing for a while. He came down out of the cave in the hills where he lived, intent only on seeing his old buddies and having a party. While he was there, he signed up for the shearing competition and enjoyed himself so much and shore so fast and so well he won the show.

Hang on a Minute

Rams are used to having their own way and often don't like to be shorn. The six foot six inches tall Munga was shearing one in Australia which was giving him a real hard time. When it was shorn and Munga and the ram had finished butting heads, Munga picked up the ram and hung it from the overhead shaft by its horns. When the cocky came in and saw it he couldn't believe his eyes. It took him and three others to get it down.

Shearing folklore

I went to sleep that night with my head full of shearing tales, looking forward to when my path crossed with that of the mighty Munga.

A Cocky Bunch of Cockies

ABOVE: Jim Morris, the poet/cocky who wears size 14 boots.

First thing in the morning at Omarama, the mist sits on the mountains like a duvet, waiting for the warmth of the sun to peel it back. We started early and travelled on through country with straight roads, flat plains and high mountains. There were few signs of habitation or life except for an old tin shearing shed which stood forlorn, waiting for those couple of weeks of the year when noise and activity would reverberate inside it.

Along the way we decided to call on a friend of Peter's, a man who was both a cocky and a poet, but who is more famous for having taken to dinner the glamorous film star Joan Collins.

I won't say where Jim Morris lives because the hidden valley is so awesomely beautiful that it is likely to get trampled underfoot as soon as people know about it. Suffice to say it is located 800 metres up "where the schist rock of Otago meets the greywacke of Canterbury." Here you can fish the pond in summer and skate on it in winter.

We turned off the main highway and drove along a winding road, hills climbing up each side and a river cutting through a stony gorge. The warming sun lifted veils of mist – the chill breath of morning – off distant mountains, revealing hues of purples and browns so subtle in their shading that, though Peter could photograph them, it would have taken Leonardo Da Vinci to have painted them.

The mountains were giants that surrounded us and yet from the road we drove along, the land fell another 12 precipitous metres to a river below. We approached a ford sign and could see where the channel was gouged out on either side of the road. The stream flowed from a waterfall that babbled over rocks, but there had not been much rain lately, so the ford was as dry as an Auckland motorway.

We first sighted our poet-cocky as a large, looming shadow through sheep pens with three farm dogs running around his heels. Jim Morris is cut from a different cloth; he wears size 14 boots, which in his day were the biggest playing rugby. A wide-brimmed hat is pulled over his face, but it is the nearby mountains that stand in his shade. He is Jack-o-the-valley.

He puts down the great lump of a fence post he has been handling like a matchstick and extends a huge hand. That's when I discover he has a finger-crushing handshake.

He stands tall and looks straight at you with a grin that is ready for anything. When he leans on something, he takes it over; when he talks the words come from deep down and embed themselves in your eardrums like friendly bullets. We shared a cup of tea with him and a yarn or two. And he showed us around his wilderness patch of paradise. At one point we drove in Peter's car across a freshly cut field of hay. The stubble scraped the underside of the car and it sounded as if we were fording the running waters of a stream.

A few years back Jim was big news worldwide because of the night he dated one of the most sought-after women in the world. Joan Collins was coming to New Zealand and would be attending a charity function in aid of cancer research. In a jocular vein, Miss Collins revealed that she did not have a date for the evening, and suggested she would like to share it with a real New Zealand farmer.

Some say Jim was chosen for his blunt charm, but he said it was because he had donated so much money to cancer research – the disease took his beloved wife Ju from him.

As the big night approached, the media blew up the "date" out of all proportion (the two were seated next to each other at a huge banquet). Then it seems Madame La Collins got cold feet. Maybe it was looking in the newspapers as if the woman who had once refused the advances of Richard Burton was hard-up for a man. The star had her publicity people put out a statement saying there had been a misunderstanding and she had wanted New Zealand "lamb" not a New Zealand "man."

When the dinner went ahead, the Hollywood star snubbed the South Island cocky and so she never found out what an interesting character Jim Morris is. He never went to Hollywood and she never became a rousie.

Nor did she get to sit on his deck and listen to his poetry as the sun snuggled down for the night in the cleavage of the distant mountains. Poor Joan. What you missed out on…

Back Country Woolshed

There's a little old red woolshed
And it's tucked beneath the hill
And it doesn't sit quite square or look too new,
And it's made of rough adzed timbers
Cut straight from standing bush
As the builders in the old days used to do.

And it's seen a good few shearers
As the years have come and gone,
And the way they work just hadn't changed at all;
For the shear blades still are flashing
As the white fleece folds away
Like old timers with their names upon the wall.

There's tar stains on the woodwork
And old tallies on the rails
And the timbers of the board are sprung and rough,
And the jumbucks still are sandy
And they make the shearers work
For the days are just as hard and just as tough.

And some would say unkindly
As they look the old shed o'er
It's kept up by the borer in the wood;
But it brings back lots of memories
And has atmosphere in heaps
Which means more to me than new sheds ever could.

Jim Morris from his book *Different Worlds – Backcountry Yarns*

OPPOSITE PAGE:
Jim's hidden valley.

We left Jim Morris' beautiful valley and drove through the Lindis Pass into Central Otago. The hills suddenly thrust up more starkly and steeply around us. When they gave way to gentler and greener inclines, we came across the sign for the historic Morven Hills Station.

We pulled off the road and drove to the top of the track and were met by a dramatic scene. Two dead deer were flying though the air before us. They had just been airlifted by a bright yellow helicopter and we watched them being dropped straight into the back of a ute where two black dogs waited.

BELOW:
The threshold of Morven Hills Station shed – worn down by the passage of shearers.

We drove past this scene along a grass track to where the Morven Hills woolshed stood as more of a monument than a building. It was surrounded by flat, yellowing paddocks bounded by trees and overlooked by tussocky hills. The air was filled with music, not the electronic type you find in the sheds, but the natural kind, provided by goldfinches in the trees.

The Morven Hills woolshed was built long ago. It has grey stone walls and a tin roof that comes down to almost head height. The only thing new about it is the concrete stone step.

The pair of doors at the entrance look like they are the original ones, with rounded handles and one of those big, old locks. The brass handle has been highly polished by the many hands that have gripped it over the years, while the paint has been baked off the doors by the sun long ago, though it still leaves a residue which shows the colour was once green. Old pieces of wood have been nailed horizontally on the inside where the bottom slats of the door are giving way like rotting teeth. The sides of the frame have old nails in them, bent and misshapen. There is no evident reason why they are there. Each holds a long forgotten story.

There are no sheep and no shearers when I go inside, and yet the empty room seems to be alive with life. The rafters and tin roof make small clinking noises as the building settles in the heat of the day. The timber uprights and posts are a seasoned tan colour and seem to whisper to you of all the sheep and men that have passed through here. A bird calls in the corner. The floorboards creak under foot.

Old handsaws are hung on the wall beside large hand auger bits and a branding iron. Also pinned to the wall is an old newspaper article which tells that Morven Hills was founded by two Scottish brothers, John and Alan McLean. They came originally from the Isle of Mull. They first farmed in the Canterbury region, then, in 1858, John McLean (who also went by the name Big Jock) heard of a tract of land that no white man had ever trodden on.

He set off to find it with a horse and pack and headed south. At the Waitaki River he met up with the Maori chief Huruhuru, who agreed to guide him. They followed an old Maori greenstone route through the Lindis Pass and they climbed the Grandview Mountains.

From this height, John McLean looked out towards Wanaka and for the first time saw the tract of land which he intended to claim. On 5 September, 1858, he was granted a leasehold of over 200,000 hectares of the land for 14 years. But there was a catch. It had to be stocked up within a certain time or he would lose it. McLean did not have the money to do that, but that didn't matter because he was a canny Scotsman.

When the stock inspector came, McLean greeted him warmly and took him to where the sheep were grazing. That night McLean invited him into his home and was very free with the whisky bottle towards his guest.

As the inspector slept soundly, McLean's men moved the sheep to another pasture. The next day the inspector was taken to count more sheep (the same sheep). That night he once more hit the whisky bottle with his host while McLean's men mustered in darkness. And so it went on, until finally the inspector went away satisfied that the run was fully stocked.

The Morven Hills shed has 38 stands – one of the largest sheds in New Zealand. In 1868 around 20,000 sheep were shorn here. Looking at the entrance doors from the perspective of the late 20th century, I assumed there were two of them to make a larger opening. But then there was more of a class distinction. The farmer was supposed to enter by one door and the other was for the shearers and shed hands.

When the season began, the men would arrive to shear, sleeping all over the place. A muster would be called and if someone didn't show up, he was given one free meal and told to hit the road. There were plenty of people looking for work and his place was quickly taken.

After shearing, the wool was carted down to the coast by bullocks. The wagons carried 30 bales of wool each weighing 180 kg. The carts crossed rivers, bogs and anything in their path.

The roads they travelled were difficult and there were few bridges. The drivers often used a few choice words to help a bullock along. One time a farmer's wife reproached a drover for his language with the words, "John, where did you learn to swear so?"

"You couldn't learn it ma'am," he replied. "It's a gift."

The canny John Mclean decided to move out when the rabbits moved in. He sold out for one pound for every sheep on the run (reputedly there were 160,000). He had done well for himself from whisky and wool.

It was with regret we left the Morven Hills woolshed. It was as peaceful as a cathedral.

OPPOSITE PAGE: Inside the shed you can almost hear the whispers and shouts of yesteryear.

BELOW: The Morven Hills Station shed nestles into the landscape.

MORVEN HILLS

Chapter 4 · DEEP SOUTH

Deep Down in the Deep South

OF DRAGONS, DEAD SHEEP AND FIRE ENGINES

The next morning we woke up at shearers' hours, four o'clock in the morning, ready for a 4.30 am start to get to Mossburn in time to go around the sheds with the local contractor Mana Te Whata.

The night before I had phoned Mana and told him we'd be with him between 10 and 11 am.

"What's the matter," he goaded. "Can't you townies get up?"

We started off in darkness and watched the world get up. We took winding roads past lakes, driving straight through wisps of white mist that had descended like clouds fallen from the sky. The road was continually crossed by darting rabbits. We hit one, which was probably about the right odds. I estimated that you could count how many cars had been on the road that morning by counting the number of dead rabbits. Finally, some time after 7 am, we pulled into Mossburn, which bills itself as the deer-farming capital of the world. We soon found the quarters which were probably the most modern in New Zealand for the simple reason that almost a year before they had burnt down.

OPPOSITE PAGE: Kylie Hamilton in action.

BELOW: The Waterloo Station gang.

At about one o' clock in the morning, after the 1998 Mossburn show, Mana was in the local pub with the rest of the adult population of Mossburn when the publican's wife told him his quarters were on fire. At first Mana thought she was joking, but soon realised the horrible truth as the whole pub emptied out into the street to watch the flames.

Mana is a member of the Mossburn fire brigade, but he didn't have his gear with him and probably would not have been allowed to help anyway – as it was his

property burning. Some people were asleep in the quarters when the fire started. The cook woke them up and got them out before suffering a heart attack. He spent two weeks in hospital recuperating and was the only casualty.

Mana had 70 people to get to work on Monday. He had no gear and no quarters for them. Some people were lodged in the fire brigade hall. The next morning Mana's wife, Vanessa, climbed into his uncle's van to drive to nearby Invercargill to pick up urgent supplies. She got just a few kilometres down the road when the radiator overheated.

ABOVE: Mana Te Whata (centre) and Jared Manihere (right) shearer and champion wool presser.

Another van had to be sent out to collect her and carry on to The Warehouse in Invercargill where they stocked up on clothes and blankets. They stocked up with shearing gear from Reid Farmers, but when that branch ran out of stock, the branch in Gore had to be specially opened up on a Sunday.

On a Shearing Shed Wall

Work when you have to,
Quit when you can,
Be your own boss,
Be your own man.

Sing to the stars,
In the night sky.
Love a good woman.
*F*** her until you die.*
Anon

Back in Mossburn, the local diner opened up and fed the workers. Local townspeople arrived with clothes and food. Another contractor, Stumpy Stirling, phoned up and donated boxes of food. All the local contractors got together and wanted to help.

The insurance Mana received for rebuilding the quarters only covered half of what it cost. Mana knew what to do though: he called in the relatives. They came down in force: his father and his cousins. Mana worked them hard too.

Peter and I shared a breakfast with Mana in the rebuilt quarters and then headed off to the first shed. Mana drove with a three-month-old golden retriever labrador pup called Simba on his lap. As we reached the top of the last hill, Simba was out and racing us to the bottom with ears flapping, floppy legs pounding, and a glint in his eye like a racehorse.

Waterloo Station is owned by John Minty, a friendly cocky with a nice line in home-made gumboots. He wears leather, lace-up boots that stop at the ankle. On top of them rest his gumboots, which have the foot cut out of them to match.

It's Kiwi ingenuity at its best. His new-style, two-piece, composite boot is more comfortable to wear than the standard, one-piece version, doesn't get so hot in summer and still keeps his socks

OPPOSITE PAGE: Shearers are always searching for the perfect cutter and comb to shear with.

dry when he has to wade through creeks.

This is a five-stand shed. They are shearing full wool (12 months) Romney ewes. One of the shearers, Joe Clarke, is what is described as a gun shearer. They are the top shearers who regularly produce big tallies in the shearing show circuit or in the sheds. It is also a name that shows they have achieved the respect of their peers.

Joe is unusual for a gun shearer. He has hair. Most shearers have close-cropped hair like basketballers because it gets hot in the cauldron of a shearing shed. Joe's hair is curly which is perhaps why, at shearing shows, he has been given the nickname "the darling of the crowd."

But he says there are two other reasons for the name. The first is because commentators like to make things up. The second is that the first year he made the final at the Golden Shears in 1990, his gear was stolen. He had to go on in the final with someone else's gear. That got the crowd on his side.

At the shows, commentators also sometimes have the problem of deciding exactly where Joe is from. That is critical when there is such an intense North/South rivalry in the shearing world.

He was born in the North Island in Rotorua, but moved to the South Island at the age of about five. For a number of years he was based in Riversdale in Southland, but now that he has a new partner (the wool handler Joanne Kumeroa), he is based in Wanganui in the North Island. However, when the North shears against the South, he is definitely a South Island boy.

> "It's a good life... if you are single."
>
> Joe Clarke, gun shearer

The star of this shed though is undoubtedly the rousie Kylie. She has a boisterous personality. She's the Liza Minnelli of the shearing sheds. Her laugh explodes out of a loud husky voice. They say if you put her

Pet Roo

In Australia we were shooting roos for fun and shot one late at night. The spotlight was on it and all you could see was these two green eyes jumping around like a frog. Little Joey had jumped out of his pouch and we were taking shots at the poor little wee thing and I said, "No, I'll take it for a pet."

So out I went, caught little Joey and named it Frog. The boss said to me, "You'd better knock it on the head because it'll never survive."

So Vanessa asked one of the locals and she got a recipe, milk and eggs and something else, and it came through all right.

Vanessa made a bag for it and we used to hang it up on the stand every day. Smoko times we used to take it down and let it hop around the board, check out all the shearers and then put it back in the pouch again. When we left, we gave it to a wildlife centre. We walked in there with little Joey and they said, "Where did you get it from?"

"Out in the bush you know."

"But how did you get it away from its mother?"

"Oh we shot the mother."

"Whoops!"

Mana Te Whata, shearing contractor

head into a bucket of water, the bubbles would keep coming, because she'd still be talking.

Her broom skates across the ground like a hockey stick; it never leaves the ground. A sweep takes the wool out of the shearer's way. She directs the base of the broom with short, sharp flicks of the wrist at the top end of the stick.

Then she quickly leans forward, straight-backed, to sort the wool, or squats on her haunches with the broom over her shoulder or across her knees. Her hands move quickly, sorting out the oddments and tossing them aside.

Then she's up again, sweeping the bulk of the wool towards the presser. If it's a big pile, she likes to give it an extra kick with her foot behind the base of the broom. At one point she tosses the wool at the pile right where I am standing. The wool flies past my ear and she puts her hand to her mouth as if to say sorry, but I don't think she means it. She has that glint of mischief in her eye.

She has a tattoo on her chest which dives down into her cleavage. She jumps on a wool bale, leaning forward, as my eyes try to decipher the tattoo. Finally, when the vibrations have stilled, I make out the shape of a dragon. Everybody knows where it starts but only invited visitors know where it ends.

Kylie was originally from Hunterville, which is near Taihape, near Lake Taupo. She started in the sheds when she was about 13. "During the school holidays I used to go out and muck around

Broken Hill

I went there for a shearing competition. They were promoting this P&A show; it was the first one they had at Broken Hill. The whole town was behind it. At the time I was champion of New Zealand at Merinos so I got a trip there. While I was there I found out something of the history of the town. When they had a dispute between themselves or others they had a boxing ring and they would fight it out. No rules – just all out. They had a jail there as well. One of the shearers actually murdered somebody and he's still in there.

Mana Te Whata, shearing contractor

because my mother was a cook for the shearers. They didn't pay me for two years, then I went on the payroll when I was 15, and then I left school at 15 to go out into the sheds."

Kylie isn't satisfied with being a rousie. She wants to become a gun shearer. During smoko she pulls a handpiece out of her bag and gets stuck into a sheep. She shears like someone who wants to be a shearer, who has the enthusiasm, but not yet the skill. There is tension in her body and so there is also tension in the sheep.

She stands slack-legged, each foot not yet in alignment with the other, her cheeks reddening, a strand of hair falling across her face. The harder she tries, the more she nicks the sheep and the higher grow the yellow, downy ridges of wool left on the sheep's body. She gets plenty of guidance from the others in the gang. In fact, just about everybody tosses a piece of advice across the shed to her, not a lot of it helpful.

If you want to know how to shear a sheep, Mana is the one to watch. He was the world champion at shearing Merinos in 1993. Mana's cousin is Zinzan Brooke, the legendary rugby player. Zinny never wanted to be a rugby player, he wanted to be a shearer.

At Waterloo Station Mana takes over from one of the younger shearers who stands nearby watching and learning. He shears with

RIGHT: Mana shears with grace and ease.

What a Friend Would Do

I went to Australia and stopped at Melbourne and my friend drove down from Broken Hill (about a 600 km drive). He picked me up from the airport because I didn't know Melbourne that well. He took me around to another guy's place in Melbourne who I hadn't met and I was to stay there the night. My friend stayed for a cup of tea, then he drove back to Broken Hill (a round trip of 1200 km). I said, "You're crazy I could have got a taxi." "That's all right," he said. "You do that for friends." I said, "I wouldn't have done it for you."

Mana Te Whata,
shearing contractor

perfect control and easy grace; his balance is so precise that if you took away the sheep, he would fall over.

It wasn't always this smooth though. He still remembers the first sheep he shore. "I was working with my uncle's gang and I asked him if I could have a shear. He kind of gave me this funny look, but later when the run was nearly empty, he called me over. I jumped on the stand and I didn't realise my uncle had a thin comb on. I went through the gate and dragged the sheep out and started shearing under the sheep's belly. I was wondering why it wasn't going through the wool and I didn't seem to be getting a grip so I pushed the shears in hard. Still nothing, so I pushed the shears in again. I pushed it in harder and then I saw blood.

"When I pulled the shears out, the sheep's guts came out with it. The comb had gone right through into the guts and opened it up. I could see a couple of lambs in there. I frantically tried to push the guts in again.

"The sheep had to be put down. I don't know who paid for it, but my grandfather [who was in charge of the gang] wasn't very happy about it. He said to me, 'Boy, you'll never make a shearer.'"

It was a couple of weeks before Mana picked up a handpiece again. His grandfather's words didn't put him off, they probably made him even more determined. Mana was not one to give up easily. As his uncle told me, "As a child Mana was a stubborn boy. He always wanted his own way."

There is something that Mana doesn't like to be widely known about though, and that is that he was born a townie. That was mainly because of an accident his father, Tupari, had when he was a child. He is now a well-known Maori carver.

Tupari was helping his grandfather cut hay with a scissors mower and cut his leg. He went to hospital, but his injury wasn't treated properly and he developed gangrene. His leg had to be amputated. For a number of years he went to school on crutches before the family could afford to go to Auckland to buy him a prosthetic leg. Then he went to college and became one of the best boxers there. He never allowed the loss to handicap him. He was a hard man and according to Mana, "his leg was very hard on my arse."

Tupari worked at the artificial leg centre in Dominion Road in Auckland for a number of years and that was why Mana was born a townie. Mana was eight when they moved to a farm up north.

As I watch Mana shearing a sheep, I appreciate that I am watching a great artist at work. There is no effort and an abundance of time available. Each stroke is smooth and sure; the flat comb of the handpiece glides easily in and out of the nooks and crannies of the sheep's body. He bends his knees, whereas many shearers keep their legs and back straight. He keeps his head up, looking as he shears, a busy but unhurried urgency about him. Some shearers, have what they call "a beautiful slow hand." There is a spirituality about how they shear. It is where technique rises to the level of art.

Fran's Tale

You meet many unique people in the shearing sheds. Fran Hamilton is one of them. I found it hard to believe he was 55 years old when he told me. Though his hair is white, he still looks physically fit and still retains a curiosity about life that a child might possess. He has done many jobs, some of them quite prominent managerial positions and has drifted back to shearing on many occasions. This is his tale:

"I left school because it was too slow and then I started working in the offices at a freezing works. Then the off season came and it was boring, so I left. In those days you could get a job anywhere you liked. I started shearing when I was 19. I always liked farms so I worked on a farm for a while, but I didn't like the people I was working for, so I worked on another farm and I liked those people.

"After a while I thought the wages were too low and then I discovered the shearers were coming, and they were not getting paid by how hard they worked, but how effective they were. I liked that idea, so I went off and learned how to shear.

"Then after a couple of years shearing I thought, 'Gee I feel

> "I've shorn a sheep with three legs in Hereford, England."
>
> Fran Hamilton, shearer

> "I was working with people who liked to work hard and took pride in their work and I came back refreshed."
>
> Fran Hamilton, shearer

ignorant and losing track of everything that is going on.' So I went to university. While I was there I got married. I needed a job so I applied to the Broadcasting Corporation. I thought the Government would pay for me to go to university, but that didn't work out, so instead I went back and forth between shearing and university.

"I got a degree in social sciences which included economics and statistics. That was what I was interested in. I didn't want to do accountancy. It was a very narrow degree in those days. I just had interests. I knew what I was interested in and I just followed my goal.

"After my degree I went back to shearing again just to have an income while I looked around what to do, then I worked for a while as a personnel manager in the freezing industry in Auckland and then as a slaughter manager.

"But I found their whole industrial relations setup was aimed at conflict.

"You weren't allowed to work hard and there were militant unions in the freezing industry and we

BELOW:
Fran Hamilton keeps coming back to the shearing life.

Dolly and Daisy and...

In England this farmer said to me, "How many sheep would they have on the average farm in New Zealand?"

So I told him a few thousand. This obviously worried him because on an English farm you might have only two to three hundred. He looked at me aghast and said, "Don't you run out of names for them?"

Fran Hamilton, shearer

had to put in hygiene regulations to comply with the EEC. It was a hassle. I had a month's leave due, so I went shearing.

"Then I decided to go to Australia because it had been really tough here for a while [economically] but from the time that I got there the Australian economy started to go downhill. In the meantime I was investing in property on the side and that went well until about five years ago when I got divorced and everything went wrong."

For a while Fran worked for Price Waterhouse, turning companies around in Australia. Then about 18 months ago, when he was in his mid-50s, he returned to shearing for the umpteenth time. While visiting his son, who lived in Sweden where he had married a Swedish girl, Fran stopped off in Chile and found love himself.

There he met the vivacious Claudia. He left to follow the shearing work and they kept in touch by letter and phone. Then, a few weeks before I spoke to Fran, they met up in Australia where Claudia had flown for a one-month holiday.

There they married, and in true South American fashion, Claudia threw her return ticket into the bin. They came to New Zealand to work as Fran followed the shearing again and Claudia, who was a social worker, quickly got trained up as a rousie. That's where I left them until I received a phone call.

"Hi it's Fran," said the familiar voice on the phone.

Shovelling English Style

They had ways of doing things in England that were amazing to Kiwis; like they'd tie the gate up with wire and have to do it up and undo it every time they went through it. I was working on this farm with another shearer and the yard outside the cowsheds was all mud and the cows used to shit in it and it was a real mess. And one day I saw the farmer shovelling it and trying to clean it up. So I said to the other Kiwi shearer, "Come here and look at this. That about sums it up doesn't it – he's shovelling shit uphill."

Fran Hamilton, shearer

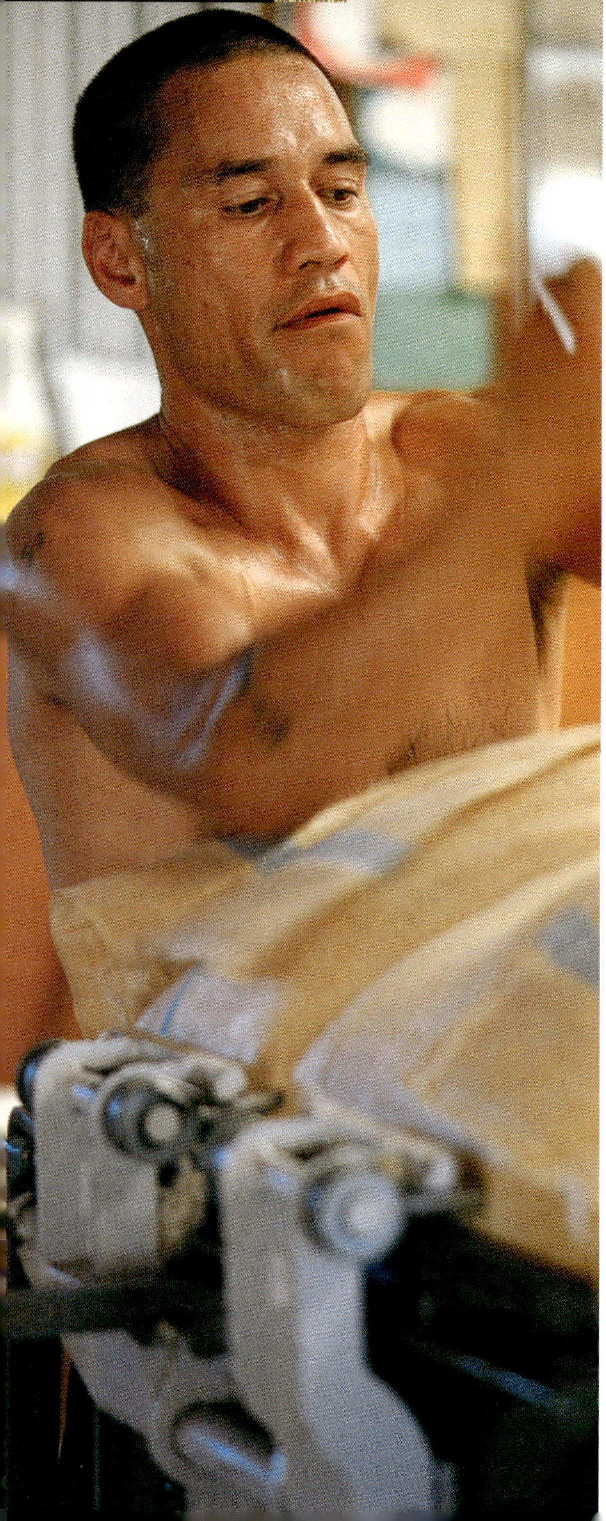

"Where are you?" I asked.

"Auckland Airport," he replied. "Do you have time to pop out and see me?"

Fran filled me in on events over coffee. I discovered Claudia had returned to Chile to be with her two children. Fran was en-route, flying back to Chile. He had intended to remain in Auckland for five days, but had second thoughts when Claudia told him how much she was missing him. She had ended the conversation by saying, "It's your birthday soon. At least let me know your number, so I can phone you."

Fran went away and changed the flight details so he would be home for his birthday. Then he phoned Claudia.

"I've got the number of where I will be on my birthday," he told her. "Have you got a pen ready?"

"Yes."

He gave her the number. She had written almost all of it out before she cried out down the phone, "But that's my number!"

The last I heard of Fran he was planning to do a season shearing in England, but then again he also had a plan to work in a Bolivian goldmine.

The Red Army Gang

From Waterloo Station we drive to a four-stand shed signposted as Glenstruan Romneys. An old tool shed stands listing in the paddock. Old tree stumps and cut-up sections of tree lie in the paddock like grotesque sculptures of nature. Rusting machinery of yesteryear stands exactly where it was last used.

A freshly killed sheep hangs in the killing block. I can see it through the wire mesh window. The sheepskin hangs on a gate, soaked in blood of a richer and deeper crimson than I

ABOVE: Joe Clarke, gun shearer.

LEFT: Intense concentration and a sheen of sweat – just another day in the shed.

have ever seen. It is matted and coagulated on the fleece, still dripping from it, staining the bottom rail of the gate and just missing a cobweb.

I nickname this gang the Red Army Gang, perhaps in honour of the spilled blood, but more practically because three of the shearers are wearing red T-shirts. Working in this gang as a rousie is yet another of the Te Whata clan, Tewhakapono. She laughs at my clumsy attempts to pronounce her name. Later, when I have managed to wrap my tongue around it, I roar it out in the style of Robin Williams in the film *Good Morning Vietnam*, "Tay-fak-a-poe-no!" She laughs at that too.

"I was born in a shearing shed," she starts to tell me.

"You mean you were brought up in a shearing shed," her cousin tries to correct her.

"I was born in a shearing shed," she repeats with a knowing smile. "I used to go to work with my mum – this is at Bill Potai's in Milton. There were eight shearers and I was only about six years old and none of the rousies showed up. It was the first time I had ever worked. Me and my auntie had to work for eight shearers and I got paid the normal wage."

However her rousieing career was interrupted by the

In the Union

One time I went along to an Aussie Shearing Union meeting. I knew half the guys. I had got to know them well through the shearing competitions over there. At the meeting they were running the Kiwis down and I thought these guys aren't going to take to me. It was Long Reach, a very staunch union town, a bit like Broken Hill. The meeting house that they were in they had all these photos of the past presidents and a couple of these guys I noticed they were in the same book that I had.

They had come over to New Zealand and they had carried on with the union. They folded here after the strike had folded and they came back here and a couple of guys – their photos were in this hall, so I thought "Gee these guys don't even know their own history." So I put them straight!

Mana Te Whata, shearing contractor

RIGHT: Mana's niece Tewhakapono Te Whata (right).

You Don't Have to be Mad to be a Presser but it Helps

One day the presser lost his cool. The cocky and the contractor were leaning over the door watching the presser pen up and he was stabbing all these sheep in the back with the knife. The cocky said to the contractor, "Get that knife off him."

And when he heard that the presser said, "Right!" and he took off after the cocky, chased him out of the shed with the knife. He was going to stab the cocky. He's chasing the cocky and the contractor's chasing him saying, "Stop, stop, put that knife down."

Now the boys were sitting on the landing eating their lunch and as they are going around the shed, the boys are shouting, "Hurry up, you nearly got him, you nearly got him, you nearly caught him."

Finally he calmed down. They could not really sack him because he would have gone off the deep end, so they had to sort of transfer him. They told him that night they were transferring him to another gang, so he went out with a huff and a puff and he went out to the contractor's vehicle and pulled off the petrol cap and shoved a rag down it and tried to set fire to it.

Andy Campbell, shearer

ABOVE: Andy Campbell, shearer and storyteller extraordinaire.

OPPOSITE: Rangi Robinson, presser.

need to go to school which she attended until the 7th form, heavily involved in culture and drama groups. What about the other schoolwork I ask her, did she enjoy that?

"Nah," is the immediate reply. She prefers real life. "Mana and Dad are teaching me how to shear," she says, then adds with a laugh. "In five years I'll be able to waste Mana."

Rangi Robinson, the presser in this gang, has the regulation number of tattoos on his body. He has a skull and crossbones with a confederate flag. He has a peacock with the words, "Born to be free." He also has an eagle which used to have a rude bit, but he's getting more respectable in his old age (41) so he decided to cover that one up.

His work is very physical and he takes a real pleasure in it. When he picks up the wool, his hands look like two giant boxing gloves. When he fleeces the wool, shaking it, he looks like a bodybuilder crunching the dumbbells. He leans forward as if he really wants to get into what he is doing.

Rangi picks up the pup Simba and tosses it playfully into the wool. Simba gives a couple of barks of protest. Then Rangi tries to bury the dog in the loose wool. When it escapes the dog decides to take refuge behind Mana.

The ganger here is PD, which doesn't stand for preventative detention but for his real name, which

ABOVE: PD takes a break.

is Peter Davidson. PD is tall, with a thin face and a moustache, long arms and legs, and a puffiness around the waist. He bends his large back instead of keeping it straight, but it's too late to correct now as he has probably shorn about half a million sheep since he started. He wears his belt loose so his arse just about hangs out of his trousers.

Shearing on the stand is very competitive and each shearer keeps an eye on the others' progress, but you don't need to do that with PD – he lets you know. As he steps over into the longblow (the long blows along the sheep's back), he slams his foot down. The harder he slams it, the better he is shearing. When the floor shakes and the light bulbs start swinging from the ceiling, the other shearers know he's on world record pace.

Hard Men and the Tender Trap

At the next shed I met Kena Te Whata, uncle of Mana and father of Tewhakapono. Though he is middle-aged and his body carries some natural padding these days, his hair is still full and black. He has wide shoulders and loose arms that can shear a sheep with easy grace. He has a broad face and a rounded nose, but it is his eyes that draw attention. They still remain the eyes of a child, attentive and still prepared, after all these years, to open wide with astonishment.

When he talks, his voice speeds up and he shifts his weight from foot to foot. He talks with his whole body, his shoulders thrown back, his hands held low at his waist, carving what he is saying from the air.

He told me about the Maori traditions, such as the one about burying the birth cord. In the old days, when a child was born and the umbilical cord was severed, the cord would be buried under a tree. That way the child always knew where its home was.

I asked him what is different about the shearers of today compared with those of the past.

"They don't have the hard men in the industry any more," he replied.

I asked him what he meant by "hard men."

"They worked all day, they drank all night and they got up the next day and they just worked. They were hard men."

But there was something more here. I kept pushing to find out what it was and Kena kept repeating the words "hard men" and shaking his head at a lost breed, until finally it clicked.

It had nothing to do with the drink. It was the fact that they got up in no fit state to work, but worked anyway. They made no excuses. They just did it. They didn't even have the idea that there was such a thing as an excuse. That was what made them "hard men."

But it's not all blood, sweat and work in the shearing sheds. The enclosed environment and the cooperative nature of the work are also a fertile breeding ground for the tender trap of love.

Most of the people involved in the shearing industry are married to or "in a relationship" with other people working in the shearing industry. It's an industry you have to work in to understand. The long hours, hard work and frequent travel are likely to destroy a relationship where the other person is an "outsider". Such relationships do exist. It just takes a lot more understanding from the other person.

Two of the lovebirds in this gang were Rose Kokiri and Clayton McGee. Rose is from Gisborne. She was brought up in the shearing world. She left it to obtain a degree in teaching people with disabilities, but she came back to it. "I can't stay out of the sheds," she told me.

She has the tattoo of a rose on her shoulder. When she was a child her older sister gave herself a tattoo. Rose told her she would tell on her unless she got one too. So her sister gave her one using a needle and Indian ink. Years later Rose had a

RIGHT: Kena Te Whata, one of Mana's uncles.

ABOVE: Rose Kokiri, rousie and mother of four.

proper one done to hide the amateur one.

Clayton McGee also came from a shearing family. His father, Clinton, is a well-known shearer in Balclutha. Clayton is tall and gangling. He looks like the ol' country boy, but he shears as smoothly as if his handpiece is sliding along glass. There are those who say he will make a gun shearer one day.

Rose and Clayton rent a house in Lumsden. Rose has three children from a previous relationship and one to Clayton. One of her children is old enough to work in the sheds, one is at boarding school, while the others are looked after by a babysitter. Later in the year, Clayton will probably have to go to Australia on his own to shear and send the money back home. It's a life that is not necessarily easy on the kids – until they are old enough to travel themselves.

We headed back to the quarters and around five o' clock the vans started returning with all the gangs. People sat around for a while, sharing jokes and drinks as the sun started to drift down towards the horizon.

The gentle burr of the shearing shed was replaced by staccato laughter and voices raised in banter and humorous protest. They talked out the problems of the day, the sheep that wouldn't lie still, the kettle that wouldn't work, the cocky who wouldn't smile. They were all a little tired, but all very satisfied. It was almost tea time and they had earned it. They had put in a good hard day's labour.

Sheep against Shearer

The shearer got mad with the sheep because the sheep was fighting back. The shearer tried to jump down on the sheep with his knees, but as fast as the shearer hit the ground, the sheep moved and he hit his knees on the board.

Claudia Hamilton, rousie

The Writer Shears a Sheep

Next morning the shearing quarters started stirring at about 5 am. That was when the first doors started squeaking and the first semi-naked bodies started heading to the showers. Knocks on doors reminded others who were still hugging their pillows about early starts. There is no false modesty here, no hushed voices. It's almost a yell, "Come on, it's nearly the middle of the afternoon."

After all, the newspaper arrives at about 5 am and the cook has been up since 4.15 am, making the breakfast and preparing the lunches that the gangs will take with them when they leave at 5.50 or 6.15, or whatever time is marked on the big white board in the dining room which is the sun, the *Bible* and CNN all in one.

Either at night before they go to bed or when they get up, everybody stares at it to see what they will be doing that day. For some, apart from road signs, it is all they will read that day.

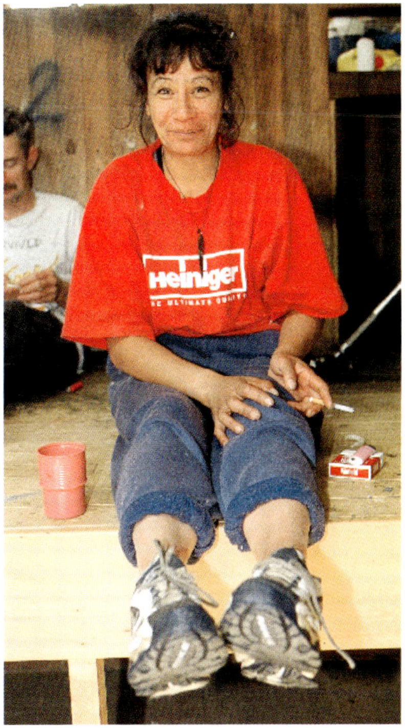

ABOVE: Rousie Hilliary Tahere.

Breakfast is the typical three-course meal that you would give a lumberjack, a cowboy or a sheep shearer: baked beans, toast, eggs and sausages and more. After they have eaten it some sit outside on the benches. The cold nips at your body at that time in the morning and the air is filled with dew that puts a haze around the distant lamppost.

Some sit with their hands in their pockets to keep out the cold. Others cradle steaming mugs of tea or roll a cigarette, contemplating the day ahead. There is not a lot of talk at this time of the morning above the distant sound of the cutlery clacking against the crockery in the dining room, other than short, barked phrases such as, "I'm going to put my broom in the car" and "Who's our presser?"

A van starts up with a guttural roar and the headlights catch the mist. Full of shadowy bodies, the van drives away into the darkness. Then another and another until the vans are all gone and only then does the sun get up.

Afterwards we drive to another farm and another shed. It's a typical shed. It keeps out the rain, lets in the sheep, and the lock on the toilet door is a piece of wire you hook over the handle.

I watch Harry Staples, who is standing in the bottom box of the press tramping down the wool. He has already set the top half in motion. It twists up and around him while he's still in the bottom

"The thing I like about this job is you never get the sack."

A shearer

half. My natural instinct is to cry out a warning. But I don't. I just watch fascinated as the top box moves inexorably towards him. It could knock him unconscious or break a limb. And he has his back to it, not looking. He just keeps tramping the wool.

The top box isn't slow. As it is about to hit him he twists, and in one fluent, unhurried movement, throws one leg over the edge of the bottom box, then the other. He bends his back and pulls himself out from between the two boxes as if he is withdrawing from the blade of a guillotine. His head is now clear of the jaws of death. The boxes clamp together. He did it without any hurry or fuss. For Harry it's just another day in the shearing shed.

Harry seems untouched by the modern world. Everything he does is natural. He hates wearing shoes, though today he is wearing them because of the nip in the air. But it's a struggle. He has trouble with his shoelace and comes over to a spare stand to sever the shoelace with a cutter. Then he pulls the shoelace out and gets hold of some old plastic fencing wire to lace up the shoe. Satisfied with that he returns to his work.

Harry has a lithe muscularity that most sportsmen would kill for. These days most people build their muscles in the gym and they lose flexibility. Harry can move in any direction at any time with full power. And he has tremendous balance. He virtually danced along the top rail of the thin metal fences inside the pens.

I suspect he lives totally by instinct, never pausing to think, just acting spontaneously in every situation. I suspect it, but I never had the chance to ask him. When I pushed the tape recorder into his face, his eyes grew as large as saucers and he made a spontaneous decision. Before I knew it the will-o-the-wisp Harry was gone.

"I went to Auckland once. I hated it. It was concrete end to end."

Mad Dog Lynch, shearer

Another natural is Judy Huri. As one of the other shearers commented, "She's easy to look at isn't she?" She looks like a model and shears like a man. She's got the type of beauty that will turn a man's head on a crowded street. She is slim-waisted in blue shearing jeans and a blue singlet. She stands straight-backed, her hair falling in a fringe over her forehead and tied in a ponytail at the back. Her lips are naturally pursed, she wears no make-up and is not trying to be beautiful.

Mana is teaching her how to shear and as she watches him I watch her. Some people only use their eyes not to bump into things, but hers are sharpened to dissect what she sees. As Mana shows her what to do, her eyes follow his hands like spotlights, recalling the deft movements and storing them away for future use.

But my enduring image of Judy will be of her leaning over the grindstone, sharpening her cutter, a lighted cigarette dangling from her pursed lips and sparks flying all around her.

Later I am relaxing to the hypnotic hum of the shearing sheds when a cry snaps me back into the present. The ebullient Kylie is calling me forward. She tosses a broom into my hand and tells me to get rousieing. It looks easy but I realise I am blind and don't know fleece wool from oddment wool. I scrabble around for a while like a demented crab.

Then another cry goes up, more of a growl this time. The sort of growl you would have heard a few hundred years ago from a bosun on a pirate ship. It is deep, wild and fierce. I look up and I am looking straight at the face of a pirate. It's a leathery face that has seen a fist or two and been creased in laughter often. It sits atop a body which is squat and muscled.

It's the face of shearer Graeme McGauhey.

"Tony, get over here," the pirate's voice rasped, "and shear this sheep for me."

This is a moment I knew would come sooner or later. No WoolPro course for me, straight into it.

RIGHT: Mad Dog Lynch.

RIGHT: Simba helps out in the shed.

Story of my life. In a few seconds I had a live sheep clutched between my thighs and the steel in my hand. I had seen enough sheep shorn by now and I followed McGauhey's instructions to the letter. And you know what? It felt like the most natural thing in the world shearing that sheep.

The only problem was I still had Mana's story ringing in my ears. I didn't want to kill my first sheep. So I didn't dig the steel in enough and had to do "second cuts" where I hadn't taken enough wool off. But I didn't do too badly for a townie thrown into the deep end; besides I was too busy to hear all the laughter that probably surrounded me.

McGauhey had made a start for me and done the difficult bits, so in future when a shearer asked me if I'd ever shorn a sheep I could give them a wink and a smile and say, "Yep mate, I've shorn half of one."

That afternoon, as a fully fledged shearer, I settled down into a corner of the comfortable, old sofa at the Te Whata Shearing Contractor's office (a converted workshop) and listened to a shearing talkfest.

This went on for about three hours and nearly all of it was about shearing.

McGauhey was there too and he did his share of the talking. In his younger days he did his share of the fighting as well. "I never used to back down to the arseholes," was how he put it. When he and his wife, Janine, were working in Australia, McGauhey's catch phrase was, "You start the engine, I'll be out in a minute."

But McGauhey is intelligent and he's a straight shooter. At the time of the Wide Comb Wars in Australia he attended a meeting to discuss the issue. It went something like this:

Wide gear v. Narrow gear

He came out with all these excuses, like they had this many second cuts and they had this many arm injuries and everything else and I said, "Who conducted the trials?"
"I don't know."
McGauhey: "Where were they conducted?"
"I don't know."
McGauhey: "Actually I'd like more information."
"We'll have an adjournment of this meeting. Graham you're not allowed back in."
*McGauhey: "What the f***"*

Chapter 5 · TOP GUNS

Top Guns & Top Girls

ABOVE: Gun shearer Paul Grainger after a stint on the stand.

TOP GUNS & TOP GIRLS

Every year in about the first week of March, the country town of Masterton which nestles in the peaceful Wairarapa becomes the destination of the finest shearers and wool handlers in the country.

The Golden Shears has been held in Masterton since 1961, when it was first won by the legendary Godfrey Bowen.

Bowen has been called the founder of modern shearing. Before he came along, shearers were shearing sheep any which way, but he refined the technique to a series of fast, economical blows. In his book on the subject, *Wool Away,* he also laid down the guidelines for competition shearing that are followed today. Nowadays the "Bowen" or "New Zealand" style has been adopted throughout the world.

RIGHT: It's all go at the Golden Shears.

The New Zealand shearing circuit runs for about six months of the year and after that many of the top guns go overseas to take part in competitions there. It was in Masterton that I was able to catch up with many of the top guns. If anybody has taken over from Godfrey Bowen as an ambassador of shearing it is Colin King, the left hander from Christchurch.

He goes by many nicknames including "The Wizard," "The Master" and "Merlin" because he is so fast he often beats men half his age. According to the official records Colin is nearly 50.

But you have to be told that fact, and even then I had to check with the man himself before I believed it. Physically he is tall, square shouldered and slightly gangly, with an intense expression on his face. He has the same purposeful look as Clint Eastwood when he's striding through his movies.

BELOW: The top guns relax in the changing shed.

MASTERTON - N.Z
9.36
CHAMPIONSHIP
DRAUGHT BEER
Golden Shears
1999
NOVARTIS

Shearing Kiwi Style

Tony Boot won the senior competition at the Golden Shears (in 1965) and at that time the prize was a trip to the Bath & West Royal show and he went with Snow Quinn. In those days the local shearers were only shearing about 60 a day and these two Kiwis, with another Kiwi, shore about 1300. In those days they had shepherds who used to drag the sheep to the shearers because they did not have catching pens and shearing boards and at the end of the day the shepherds were exhausted.

Fran Hamilton, shearer

These days he works as a shearing instructor, passing on his knowledge to those who may one day compete against him. No matter how young they are he will probably beat them.

Another star of shearing is Dion Morrell. Of all the shearers, he has the widest shoulders and the best strut, the steady and confident walk of a champion.

When he's shearing he has a smooth, flowing Maori hand. The ancestor who gave him his surname was Jean Morrell, who arrived in New Zealand last century on a whaling ship. He liked what he saw and stayed, living with the Maori who could not pronounce his name and so called him Honi. This was later apparently changed to "Horny," because he took more than one wife.

Horny Morrell would not have known at the time that he was starting a line that would one day produce a world record holder. Dion holds the record for shearing 507 Merino ewes in nine hours.

"My father was a shearer," Dion told me. "I wasn't going real flash at school and he thought I might have been better out in the work force, so he just drafted me off into the shed – and he was right. I started mucking about the sheds rouseabouting when I was about 12 and I liked being out there. I wasn't really interested in school any more."

Another record holder is Grant Smith. He's also a South Island boy "Rakaia born and bred" as he puts it. In 1994 he set a two-stand record for Merino wethers with that fellow again, Barry Taylor, the legendary Munga.

The world record attempt was decided in a typically casual manner as Grant explained. "The year before I had done a solo on the Merino ewes and near

BELOW: Gun shearer Dion Morrell.

Christmas time, after I'd done it, we were having a few beers and got talking and said, 'I will if you will,' sort of thing.'"

But where was Munga? He was not entered in the open shearing competition. When was I finally going to get the opportunity to meet this character?

Another South Islander and world record holder I did meet was Darin Forde. He has the perfect build for a shearer. Not tall, but built like an athlete, with broad shoulders.

He is from a family of seven brothers, five of them shearers. "When I turned seventeen I started shearing because my brother had a shearing run. It was on my mind because the oldest brother was doing quite well at the shearing at the time. They were making good money so I thought I'd better have a go. The first day I sheared 95." By the time of his world record, Darin shore 720 ewes in nine hours.

"When I go to a show I look back and try to see where I went wrong and where I can go better. I get my wife to video me and then I look back and say, 'I'm doing that blow wrong.'"

Mighty Munga

One day we were shearing these tough sheep at Morven Hills and they are pretty renowned for their toughness. I had a real good sheep in my pen and I left it in there on purpose. I went in there one time and it had gone. Munga had reached over and grabbed it off me.

Grant Smith, gun shearer

"Shearing is the same old thing to some people, but every sheep is different, every shed is different, you are working with different people all the time."

Johnny Arnold

Johnny Arnold probably wouldn't be called a gun shearer yet. He looks like he could be handling a different sort of gun. He sports one of those old-fashioned sergeant-major moustaches; his head is shaven like a squaddie and there is a parade ground march to his walk. He is one of those prodigal sons who left shearing only to return when he found life didn't match up to what he already had.

"I gave up one season when I was 18 and tried the fast lane life in Auckland. I just wanted to try something new in my life. I was forklift driving and doing store work. The job was boring. I was doing the same old thing all the time, day in day out."

Who Sheared the Sheep?

Mana and I were in the same team in Gisborne that had about six or seven shearers and Mana was on the learner's stand. Sometimes he'd be put off and he'd be pressing or cleaning up and I'd be doing the wool. When five o' clock came the shearers would leave the shed and Mana and I would get on the stands and shear for an hour before tea. We used to put the sheep down a porthole and it wasn't until about five years later that he was teasing me and he was telling me that he always got the sheep counted out onto his tally and he got paid for them. He thought it was great getting paid for my sheep!
Jills Angus Burney,
gun shearer (retired)

Another world record holder I encountered at the Golden Shears was Jills Angus Burney. She has shorn 548 sheep in a day, the highest tally achieved by a woman. She is a woman who has been successful in what is traditionally a man's arena and this is her tale.

"I grew up in the Manawatu at Feilding with an adopted family called Burney. When I was older I tracked down my birth family at the top of the South Island and they are called Angus.

"My brother, who's about three years older than me, went pressing as a young lad and got me a job rousieing when I was 14. I learned to shear when I was 14 and I did my first full day when I was 16. I did 48 ewes in a nine-hour day and I was told to stop at four o'clock because I had blisters so big on my hand I couldn't hold the handpiece.

"The contractor told me I wasn't allowed to keep shearing because I'd probably cut myself, so I packed a sad, dropped my bottom lip and started crying because I wanted to finish the day. I wanted to get over 50 and I didn't want to be told to stop. The blisters were so big on my hand I couldn't hold a pen when I went back to school the following week. It was the best way of getting out of schoolwork I'd ever found.

"I left school in the seventh form to go crutching and rousieing in the South Island, and I did that when I was 19. I got a job three months later shearing for Jeff Fagan in Te Kuiti. That was my first stand and I think I did about 130 then.

"I shore at the Golden Shears for the first time in 1980. They had too many entries so they turned some of us juniors down. I got to shear because a woman shearer called Barbara Marsh, who was my mentor at that time, got me to shear for someone else who couldn't make it. The other person was a Maori girl and as I was shearing I was scared that someone would come up to me and say, 'You're not this woman with a Maori name.'

"Once you start doing well gender comes into it. When you start doing really well, male egos get in the way. The Australian men used to be so dumbstruck that a girl was on a handpiece fulltime that they would give you a lot of respect.

"I remember one year I was in Australia and my boyfriend was a young New Zealand guy and he got teased about me being a better shearer than him. In the end we broke up and I don't know if that had some impact on him. It was hard for him. He was a nice lad, I was very fond of him, but I was a better shearer.

"When I was shearing in Alexandra, I was working for a contractor down there that had a fairly rough team and I came home one night from the pub and I got my jaw broken by a shearer because I had beaten him that day. I'd shorn about 240 of these quite tough winter shearing sheep and he'd shorn about 230. He'd gone to one pub and I'd gone to another, and the pub that I went to we had a good time, and the pub that he went to they teased him for being beaten by a girl. I was already in bed and there was no one else in the girl's room, and he came in and pulled me out of bed and told me that if I wanted to be one of the boys I had to stay up and drink with them. He broke my jaw on the pool table."

"Why would a woman want to shear when it's a dirty, smelly job?"

"It's a skill. There is no difference between riding horses and shearing sheep. People who get out there and do equestrian – that's a smelly, dirty thing to do too!"

Jills Angus Burney, gun shearer (retired)

Poetry in Motion

When Mana Te Whata was living in Alexandra and we were shearing in the open together, I used to go over there and he had this bean bag shaped like a sheep. And Mana and I would get it and we would draw pen marks on it for the blows of a sheep and people used to think we were crazy. I did Tai Chi and Mana and I used to talk about the poetry and the motion and the balance and the beauty of shearing. When you see a guy shearing really fast it's poetry in motion, especially the Maori guys like Larry Lewis and Samson Te Whata, who are probably the two most fluid, beautiful-to-watch shearers I have ever seen in my life. David Fagan is a Pakeha technician. He doesn't have flow. Dion Morrell has got it and Mana has got it.

Jills Angus Burney, gun shearer (retired)

OPPOSITE: Barry "Munga" Taylor, gun shearer and personality.

On the Saturday night of the Golden Shears, New Zealand took on Australia in a shearing test and I got my first sight of Barry "Munga" Taylor. He is so tall it looks as if he needs to duck his head under the crossbar when going through the gate to collect his sheep. He is long limbed with straggled hair that falls almost to his shoulders. The height and the hair reminded me of all those Tarzan movies. Mighty Munga, Lord of the Jungle.

Even before the test starts he has already stamped his personality on the proceedings. He rejects a Merino sheep from the pen. The referee seems perplexed, so Munga grabs the ewe in question and starts to shear it. Whether this was to show the judge he could not possibly have shorn it properly is uncertain. By now it's too late. The sheep has to be rejected anyway because Munga has got a head start on it.

"Barry Taylor was selected as lock for the All Blacks but they wouldn't let him play because he was too tough."

Next it transpires that they have run out of Merinos because they only brought enough for the test. There's no replacement for the one Munga has rejected. To even up the playing field each of the competitors has to drop one of their Merinos.

Then the Aussies, who are used to shearing Merinos, complain that the Kiwis have an unfair advantage. So now each of the competitors has to drop a crossbred ewe too. If they keep going like this there won't be any sheep left to shear.

And all this mischief was created by Munga.

During the delay the commentators try to keep the audience amused by telling Munga tales. Finally we get started. Barry Taylor has a long way to lean, but he also has a lot to lean with. With his help, New Zealand wins the test. By chance I blunder into the reception afterwards and suddenly find an enormous figure looming over me.

It can only be Munga. I quickly discover he has a quick grin and a loud laugh (like a sheep that's just drunk a keg of beer). He tends to talk in short, sharp sentences accentuated by bobs of the head. I asked him where the nickname Munga came from.

"I don't know. I do know, but I can't say. I have a good time. How's that?"

He paints his life story quickly with broad brushstrokes.

"I had sheepdogs you see and off season I knew a lot of shearers. I used to go in the sheds penning

ABOVE: Dean Ball checks out the competition sheep.

up and pressing. I did that for a while. I knew how to shear on the farm, but I had never done it for a living. Then, doing the pressing work, they used to get me on the stand and I used to love it because I did it just as fast as them, even though I didn't do it for a living. And then when it came to the crunch and I was 24, I started shearing for a living and away I went.

"It was a hard school. I wasn't told what to do; I was kicked and punched and made to do it. I never went to shearing school. I watched other shearers and picked it all up in the sheds."

The man from Oamaru travelled the world eight times on the shearing circuit and then suddenly encountered the two m's – marriage and mortgage.

"Get married, get a mortgage, life's all over."

"That's when I gave up shearing. I went to the freezing works. I didn't like the freezing works. The freezing works is not a place for a shearer because shearers like working. You go to the freezing works, you don't work. I was a butcher; I was doing the pelting; I had seven different jobs. Being a shearer you want to just work. That's what you do. So I quit. I said, 'Bugger this' and I went back to shearing again.

"I went to America shearing. Came home from there and I bought the sheep dipping business and I'm still married and I've still got a mortgage."

In his own inimitable way Munga unlocked another piece of the shearing puzzle for me. These days you don't have to work to make a living. The Government will happily pay you to sit at home and watch daytime soap operas. But most of us feel the need to work to make money to somehow justify our existence. A shearer not only has to work, he *has* to work hard. That is really what sets them apart.

Barry Taylor is shearing tonight despite a serious car accident. As he was driving here tonight he crashed his car into a lamppost. The car's a write-off and so is the lamppost. Barry hit it but bounced off and kept running.

Commentator at the Golden Shears

Wool Handlers Extraordinaire

At the Masterton Civic Centre, which houses the Golden Shears, there is an unwritten rule that the (mostly male) shearers sit in the stands on one side of the stage, while the (mostly female) wool handlers sit on the other. I sat with the girls. And the babies.

One-month-old Taine Te Whata was there pretending to be asleep. His mother, Vanessa Te Whata, had brought him along, ostensibly because she wanted to have another shot at the Golden Shears wool handling title. I knew the real reason he was there was to absorb the sounds and the ambience of the Golden Shears.

Mana and Vanessa met in the shearing sheds. Was it love at first sight over the wool bales? Not quite. The beginning of their relationship was when Mana accidentally cut Vanessa's hand. Vanessa didn't make the kindest remark to him then. They have now been married 14 years and have three bright-eyed children, so perhaps all courtships should begin with a bloodletting ceremony.

Vanessa is a country girl who wanted to become a stock agent. Before she applied there had been another female stock agent who had been a little too free with her favours. So Vanessa didn't get the job because the company now had a policy against employing female stock agents. Vanessa sent them a letter which gave them short shrift and she went into the sheds instead.

BELOW: (from left) Billy Greenshields, Gina Nathan and Vanessa Te Whata, first, second and third in the wool handling championship at the Golden Shears.

RIGHT: Tina Rimene, champion wool handler in 1997.

Vanessa knows how to give short shrift when it's needed. She gets to the point more quickly than anyone I have met and she has no pretensions at all. When she and Mana were working in Australia, according to Mana her forthright honesty used to get her into trouble. But Vanessa simply calls a spade a spade. If it's a shovel, she calls it a shovel. What's wrong with that?

She has a way of asking questions that is unlike anyone I have ever met. When she really wants to know the answer she will wrap her tongue around a simple word like "Why?" – twisting it into a sidewinder missile that starts deep inside her and comes out with increasing velocity.

Vanessa didn't have any babysitting problems at the Golden Shears. Little Taine had a score of "aunties" and slept snuggled in a variety of female arms. The chief babysitter was Barbara Newton, who is a wool classer, wool handling judge, photographer and general enthusiast for the industry.

"The shearing industry is the most underrated work force," she told me. 'They sweat their guts out; they are the only people who take a towel to work because they sweat.

"I think the wool handlers get a bum steer from the shearers. They used to be the people who just took the wool away, but really a wool handler is far more versatile than a shearer and there are more skills involved in what they are doing. A shearer has just got to know how many blows it takes to blow out a sheep and then, 'Hello, we're off. Where's another one?'

"A wool handler has got to sort it out. No fleece is the same, they have to make decisions about what they are going to do about it.

"Originally I wanted to be a scientist. Always had wool around the house and I love the feel of it. You get the passion and I just love the lifestyle and most of all I like the people. I am in the shed four months of the year for the pre-lamb, and the rest of the year I'm at home with another lot of people, and the people I have met in the sheds are just a different set of people; different values and different attitudes."

On the stage are four large wool handling tables that are about the size of small trampolines. The shearers are on another stage about four feet higher. They provide the fleeces for the wool handling competitors to work on. The wool handler picks up the fleece as gently as if it is a baby and tosses it gracefully onto the table. The greater the elegance with which the fleece lands on the table, the greater the cheer from the spectators.

Around me the other competitors shout advice and encouragement. Just about all the wool handlers know each other. Most of the calls in this heat are for Miriam Haig who is on table four.

Miriam is full of energy. Even when watching from the stand she doesn't stop moving – chewing

WALLACE BAIN
LAW OFFICE

gum, smoking, constantly expressing herself with her hands and her face. She is in perpetual motion.

But she also has the skill to listen and when she understands what you are saying, her answers are snappy. A double "yes" is like the crack of a whip. There's a feminine softness to her face and yet a tough, inner core. She has all the skills to have become a successful actress if she hadn't first fallen in love with wool.

"It was never anything different to what it was going to be," she told me. "From 12 or 13 I wanted to be a wool classer, even though I didn't know anything about it; that's what I wanted to do. I was a tomboy as a kid. I always hung around with Dad on the farm. My sister was a wool handler when I was at school and I decided that was what I wanted to do and I just did it."

Miriam stayed on at school long enough to do bursary and university entrance. So I put it to her that she could have got her degree and found some quiet little office job somewhere.

"No," she said with a dismissive shake of the head. "No, I'm not interested in office work at all. It's boring. You do the same thing every day and it's the same people, you don't get to travel. This is a real travelling job and you get to meet a lot of neat people."

I don't ever recall having been in the middle of a group of women before. They continually turn and twist to talk to each other even as they scream at the stage. In the lulls they offer advice and compare scores.

"Hey how much did you lose on the board?"

"Don't take out too much yellow."

"I got 29, how many did you get?"

"Forty-seven."

"They're a bit bloody harsh aren't they."

All through this children wander and play in the aisles. A shaven-headed woman sitting next to a man with dreadlocks picks a child up by his collar and moves him along. There is so much energy all around me and I feel as if I am sitting in the middle of a volcano.

BELOW:
Grinding gear for the next shear.

Just along from me is Joanne Kumeroa, generally recognised as one of the top wool handlers of the moment. She is tall, angular, concentrated and intelligent. Too intelligent for some.

"I started in the sheds when I was 13. I was too

clever for the teachers, so they said I could go. I got dismissed for giving the teachers a hard time. My dad started me off. He's got a run in Wanganui. When I was 14 he took me down the South Island and left me down there and told me to find my own way back and my own money and that worked really well."

On being at the top of her profession she told me, "I try and keep a clear head. That's really hard to do when there's a lot of pressure put upon you. I used to feel pressure, but now I ignore that and my motto is that I try and start again at each show. It's a new beginning for me and I never try and be where they put me up. I think if I paid attention to what everybody said I wouldn't be up where I am now. I just try and keep a low profile for myself."

The tall and androgynous Gina Nathan started wool handling when she was 14. "I went out for a ride with my uncle on the run and we actually went out to take groceries for the gang, but when they woke up in the morning there was no one there so I had to get up and I've been there ever since."

Robyn Murray also started early.

"I was a school dropout. I didn't do very well at school because I didn't want to. I went on a holiday to Australia and when I came back I got a job in Kawhai. I hated it. I didn't like the dags (sheep droppings that catch on the wool at the rear) but then the money was good. When I started I was getting $4.50 an hour (17 years ago) and that was good money for a 16-year-old. The money kept me attracted and then the lifestyle. I love it. I have travelled all around New Zealand and I would not have done that had I not been in the shearing industry."

Got a Bed for the Night?

I know people in just about every town in New Zealand. Very rarely do we need hotel accommodation because we have set up a network from the bottom of the South to the top of the North. There are about two towns where we have to get a hotel.

Robyn Murray, wool handler

Wool handling is very physical. It's been described as an eight-hour aerobics session. Tina Rimene, who won the Golden Shears Open Championship in 1994 and again in 1997, compares the job with when she played softball for Wairarapa.

"It was on a par. I'd rather do wool handling. You do something and you know you can do it better the next time around and you can't wait to have another go. And the next one you have another go at it and you get better and better and you put it into competition. I am always learning. I learn off the juniors, the seniors… I could learn off a learner."

One of the more experienced wool handlers is George Mason, whom everyone calls Oti, a nickname that stuck as a toddler. He was the Golden Shears wool handling champion in 1996 and represented New Zealand at the world championships in Ireland in 1998, where he came third. He has been working in the shearing gangs for 33 years.

"The very first day I stepped into the shed, aged 14, the broom was put in my hand," he told me. He's been wool handling ever since, apart from a couple of years pressing. So why didn't he become a shearer? Surely that would have given him more money and more prestige.

Oti gave me a knowing smile.

"I've never been interested in shearing. I can remember Mavis Mullins making the same comment: 'Once you touch wool and you grow to love it, you just can't leave it alone.'"

The wool handlers are quiet for the first time as the names are announced for the semifinals. Everybody listens intently and then there are kisses all around for those who are through.

Vanessa Te Whata made it through to the final on the Saturday evening. So did Teena McLaren, who'd been the junior wool handling champion in 1997. She didn't have the problem Vanessa had of breastfeeding baby Taine half an hour before the final started. That problem was imminent because, though she didn't look it, the rumour was that Teena was nine months pregnant. Of the other two finalists, Gina Nathan was not pregnant and bearded Billy Greenshields definitely wasn't.

BELOW: Alan "Mickey" MacDonald hangs around while Dean Ball has a drink.

The four competitors came out for the final. All had different coloured baskets – red, blue, green and white to put their oddments in. Vanessa was at the far end with the red baskets. Teena was blue, Gina was green and Billy was white at the near end. They all nervously adjusted the position of their baskets.

This was the big one. Wool handling has only been an event at the Golden Shears since 1985 and in that time only nine names had appeared on the trophy. Who would be the tenth?

Each wool handler had a shearer shearing their sheep for them. As soon as the shearers started, the wool handlers were on their knees, their hands poised ready to grasp the first tuft of wool that fell away.

I watch Vanessa as she prowls her table with her head down and shoulders hunched. She plucks the oddments out and tosses them into the basket. When she considers the fleece is ready she rolls it and places it in the wool bale. When all the fleeces are done and the oddments sorted, she grabs her broom and cleans up under the table and around the floor. Then, breathless and reddening, she thrusts her hand into the air to notify the judges she has finished.

She is first on the floor and waits for the others to finish. They do one by one until only Gina Nathan is left. She seems to take an age to finish. All the other competitors are sitting exhausted, watching her. The whole audience is watching. She goes on and on, fussing here and there, almost making a show of it now she has centre stage. The commentator tries to fill the time by explaining how important quality control is for the future of the industry – until at last Gina puts both hands up with an expressive shrug and the final is over.

We had to wait even longer for the result. Long enough for the competitors to shower and change, long enough for them to agonise over what they would have done differently. Strangely, the winning sequence ran in perfect order from least pregnant to most pregnant.

It was the bearded Billy Greenshields who added his name to the trophy. Despite and perhaps because of her dawdling, Gina Nathan was second when the quality points were added up. Vanessa was third, so her long journey from the Deep South with baby Taine wasn't in vain. Teena McLaren was fourth. One day she'd be able to tell her child how it took part in the Golden Shears before it was born.

RIGHT: South Islander Darin Forde is a world record holder.

Chapter 6 · TE KUITI

Journey to the Centre of the Universe

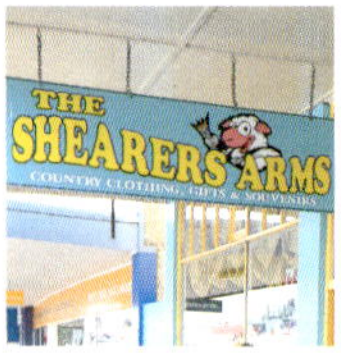

JOURNEY TO THE CENTRE OF THE UNIVERSE

Te Kuiti, a small rural town of about 4000 people in the King Country, lays claim to being the Shearing Capital of the World. In fact it feels like the centre of the world after you have driven along winding country roads to get there.

There are other towns in New Zealand that might make the same claim: Masterton, home of the Golden Shears, and Alexandra and Gore in the South Island. Some people say they don't have real sheep in Te Kuiti, which has mainly crossbreds. A large number of the sheep in the South Island, and indeed the world, are Merinos. They produce finer wool, which is more difficult to shear.

Te Kuiti does have a right to the name Shearing Capital of the World as the region has produced three individual world shearing champions (in crossbred machine shearing). They are David Fagan, Alan MacDonald and Brian "Snow" Quinn. Pretty impressive when only four other men have won the world championships (two of them Kiwis).

OPPOSITE PAGE: The imposing statue at the entrance to Te Kuiti, the Shearing Capital of the World.

Standing in Rora Street, the main street of Te Kuiti, looking out at the green hills that form a continuous, jagged fringe along the horizon, it is possible a child might believe Te Kuiti was the whole world. But I would go further and say that Te Kuiti is the Shearing Capital of the Universe.

On my first night there the sky appeared to be a quilt of glittering stars. There were so many stars I was unable to count them. For the first time I really understood the magnitude of the universe we inhabit. And, as it happened to me in Te Kuiti, it stands to reason that Te Kuiti must be the centre of the universe.

It definitely is for the locals early in April when the New Zealand Shearing Championships are held in the Waitomo Cultural and Arts Centre, which is just down King Street. You pass underneath a Second World War commemorative arch and over a bridge which crosses a babbling river and there it is.

Though the competition is centred here, the whole town takes part in what is known locally as the Te Kuiti Muster. Friday night is Muster Market Madness when the main street is closed off for a family festival. It's a night when teenage girls wear their best clothes and walk hand-in-hand with their boyfriends; when old friends meet in the street with hugs; and new babies are fussed over. It is a night of laughing children, fairground rides, blaring music and steaming hot dogs with dripping tomato sauce.

Just as other shops bring out Christmas trees, the Te Kuiti shops are filled with representations of sheep and shearing in the form of sheep dolls, sheep rocking horses, ribbons and cups from past championships, cut-out, sheep-shaped trestles with wool glued on them, and a granny sheep with glasses and a hat.

And the shopkeepers get sillier than that. One put assorted sheep shearing gear in their shop window on top of some wool bales with chocolate drops scattered all around. The sign said, "Guess how many sheep droppings in the window and win a $20 voucher!"

On Friday night the strongman competition is held. No, this has nothing to do with pressing, more to do with pulling. A row of trestles with lumps of wood nailed about two metres apart is laid out on Rora Street. Lying on the trestles with their size 14 boots pressed against the blocks are two opposing teams of bulky looking blokes and one or two women.

Threaded between them is a rope about 8 cm thick. The timekeeper counts down, "Three, two, one," and both teams take the strain. The man at each end (who usually weighs about 150 kg) has the added advantage of being able to twist his body and sink his teeth into the last block of wood for extra purchase.

On the Saturday there is a street market with four Fred Dagg lookalikes in black gumboots, black singlets and bush hats, wandering around singing songs, enacting an ancient gumboot throwing ceremony and doing some strange cocky's haka.

Back in the hall there was a real haka. When Hendrix Paahi won the junior shearing championships, four of his "cuzzies" charged onto the lower stage and did an impromptu haka. It was the whole chest-slamming, foot-stomping routine, with Hendrix joining in on the upper stage. When it finished the whole crowd erupted in boisterous acknowledgement.

There was another sweet moment when Veronica (Ronnie) Goss won the open New Zealand wool handling title and was presented with a bouquet of flowers. As she left the stage she was mobbed by three girls – her young daughters, their little fingers reaching out to touch the flowers.

Rodney Macdonald came third in the senior shearing championship (for shearers who have recorded a tally of 310 to 410 sheep in a nine-hour day). Rodney usually goes by any nickname that starts with "Big". "Big Bad Rodney Macdonald" is the usual variation. He's the same size as a member of the Mongrel Mob, with a big belly overlapping his belt and tattoos on his arms. Big Bearded Rodney looks rough, tough and mean, but appearances can be deceptive because he shears with a lovely, smooth hand. Later I observed him politely introducing his fiancée to his friends and I suspect "Big Bad" Rodney might be a bit of a gentleman on the quiet.

He's a northern lad (Raglan) who is going to make more of a name for himself as the years go by. One who already has is the "Tuakau Flyer" – Digger Balme. The unusual first name is courtesy of his brother via his grandfather and started with his parents. If you are confused I'll let the Digger explain.

"I was christened Richard. My grandfather always wanted to call me Dick. He said he wasn't calling any grandson of his a poofter name like Richard, so he called me Dick and then my brother couldn't say Dick so he said Dig and the name has stuck ever since."

Digger is one of the characters of the shed, never short of a joke. He used to be a speed merchant, throwing the steel into the wool like there was no tomorrow, but then he decided he had better get serious about his shearing and get some quality. Based just south of Auckland, he found a lack of "good, hard shearers to race against in the sheds" so he moved to Te Kuiti where he joined up with the world champion David Fagan.

It paid off in January when he was part of a three-stand world record with fellow Te Kuiti-based

shearers, Roger Neill and Dean Ball. Dig achieved a new individual record of 621 lambs.

Another local lad who knows something about world records is Alan "Mickey" MacDonald. Mickey has also been world champion, is a shearing contractor and a real character. He shears like a little buzz saw and walks as if he is on springs. Mickey is like one of those wind-up toys that never stops. Except you don't have to wind him up. He does that himself.

He started off as a town boy but adds with a twinkling smile, "Piopio is only just a town, it's not as big as Los Angeles." For the record, Los Angeles has a population of about eight million, Piopio about 500.

"I've been shearing for 20 odd years," the Piopio Kid told me. "The first thing that attracted me to shearing is you got paid for what you did. Like, if you were working with someone and you both had a shovel each and you were working harder than the other fellow on an hourly rate, you just got paid the same as him and I hated that, I've always attacked my work.

"I did my first few seasons in North Auckland and from there travelled to Australia and Britain in the off seasons. The most time I've had off in that time was with a chainsaw industry in 1994. In that time I've done four nine-hour lamb records – the first one 768, I think it was. The next one was 800 and that was combined with a two-stand with David Fagan in which we did 1603. The next one I did was 805 and David came back the year after and did 810, and I came in the year after in 1993 with 831, and that's where it sits now."

That night Mickey came second in the New Zealand championships. The man who beat him was David Fagan. The house in Te Kuiti where I stayed used to be owned by David. It is on top of the hill with sweeping views of the valley so that looking down you feel like the King o' the Hill. There is no doubt that David Fagan is the King of Te Kuiti.

He is a master shearer, perhaps the best ever on crossbreds. He has honed his technique down to clinical perfection.

Unlike most shearers, who push their shorn sheep down the porthole while they are still standing, David doesn't allow his sheep to stand. They remain on the board until their heads are halfway through the porthole. By the time they clamber to their feet there is only one way to go.

"When he started David Fagan was a competitor. Now he's a champion. I don't think there is any better athlete in New Zealand."

Colin King, "Merlin"

OPPOSITE PAGE:
Big "Not So Bad"
Rodney Macdonald.

ABOVE: Former All Black and Te Kuiti farmer Colin Meads (left).

OPPOSITE PAGE: Champion shearer David Fagan has a flawless technique.

In shearing sports you have to take the least time and incur the least penalties. David is a minimalist. No movement is wasted. He is also minimalist in appearance; with no hair and no fat, and no bulky muscle, unlike many of the other shearers.

He even has the awards walk onto the stage (an action he has repeated many times) down to perfection. He takes short, efficient strides, smiles, grabs the microphone, gives a few thanks, then hands the microphone back, and tries to hang on to all the trophies and prizes without dropping any of them.

I thought back to the Golden Shears. David Fagan's name first appeared on the honour roll at the Golden Shears in 1982 when he won the Young Farmers Club blue ribbon event. His first open title was in 1986. That same year he won his first world title, sharing the pairs crown with Ric Pivac at a special world championships held in Australia to coincide with the America's Cup.

He won his first world singles title in 1988, retained it in 1992, but was beaten in Wales in 1994 by the Piopio Kid, Alan MacDonald. Then David took the title back in 1996 and successfully defended it in 1998 at Gorey, Ireland, which makes him the reigning world champion.

But after David's first Golden Shears open win in 1986, Colin King worked his magic and won it for the next two years. Then Edsel Forde took the title before David was finally able to win it again in 1990. After that he never gave it back, winning it nine years in a row until the 1999 championship.

> "You can't beat him on speed, you can't beat him on quality, you can't beat him in the head... He's an all round champion."
>
> Godfrey Bowen, "The Original"

In 1999 he made the final again. Would he win 10 in a row or would someone snatch his crown? In the semifinal David was matched blow for blow by Hamish Mitchell, but the Scotsman lost out on quality. In the DB national championships (which included a mix of Merinos and crossbreds) preceding the open final, David struggled on the Merinos. His zippy style was not suitable for the tougher wool. He fell a whole sheep behind the pace and could not make up time on the crossbreds.

NZ OPEN SHEARING
CHAMPIONSHIP
FINAL
NEW
SHEARING
heiniger

He finished fifth and looked a little tired, with the open final just a couple of hours away. Uneasy lies the shearer's head that wears the crown.

The young and not so young guns were lining up to shoot him down.

On stand one was Dean Ball from Te Kuiti. With short hair and a moustache, he looks like an SAS soldier with a compactly muscled body ready for battle.

On stand two was Darin Forde, the world recorder holder from Winton and the only South Islander in the final. He had just beaten David Fagan to take out the DB national championship.

On stand three was the King himself. As usual the rest of the world did not seem to exist for him. He was aloof and focussed on the task ahead.

On stand four was John Kirkpatrick, the man from Pahiatua who won the intermediate title in 1993, the senior in 1994 and whose dream was to one day win the open. Would this be the year?

On stand five was Paul Grainger, a man who had already won the Golden Shears title back in 1985. Could the tall, balding Te Kuiti man win it again 14 years later?

On stand six was yet another King Country man, Roger Neil from Piopio, who had shared in the three-stand world record with Dean Ball and Digger Balme in January.

The hall was buzzing as the six competitors went into the pens to check the 20 sheep they would have to shear. These were nervous moments for all. Finally they were all back out on the board, each leaning forward with his left hand on top of the gate.

"Timekeepers ready," the announcer's voice boomed around the arena.

"Judges ready."

"Competitors get set – Go!"

And we're off. Six gates are flung aside, six sheep are dragged out onto the board and six handpieces are buzzing furiously.

Fagan does his first sheep in 44 seconds. Forde, the South Islander, comes back at him and gets his third sheep down the chute first. Fagan is now four blows behind. Forde is still ahead as he reaches for his fifth sheep first. "Fasten your seat belts ladies and gentlemen," screams the commentator. "We are in for a ripsnorter."

Fagan catches up on the seventh sheep, prompting more eloquence from the commentator.

OPPOSITE PAGE: "Mickey" MacDonald throws the steel into another sheep.

"David Fagan now has sparks coming out of his nostrils."

At 10 sheep, the halfway mark, Fagan is a quarter of a sheep ahead. Forde grits his teeth and starts to pull back. On the 12th sheep he's back in the hunt, getting his in the pen one second before Fagan. He gets the 13th in first as well. Is this going to be his night? Is a South Islander going to win the open for the first time this decade?

By sheep 15, Fagan is motoring again. Now he gets his sheep down one second before Forde. Standing next to each other, they are matching each other blow for blow. They look like two images of the same reflection, their elbows rising and falling as one. There is nothing at all to separate them.

Then on sheep number 16, with just four more to go, Forde is two blows ahead. One sheep later, Fagan gets his in the pen first. Now he goes into that famous overdrive when he doesn't seem to be shearing, as much as just stripping the fleeces off the sheep. He gets four or five blows ahead to the shouts and whistles of the crowd.

But Forde digs deep and catches up and suddenly both are on the last sheep. Again they are matching each other blow for blow. The crowd goes wild as Fagan gets his last sheep in by just three blows. As Fagan pushes his time clock, Forde seems to do an additional blow of the sheep's rear – one for luck.

BELOW: Competitors down welcome cans of beer after the competition.

Then he too pushes his time clock and stands upright. Both men are blowing and drenched in sweat. For them the final is over, but there is still the quality to be judged and we still don't know who has won. The whole crowd waits half an hour for the results. A table full of silverware is carried out onto the stage. Speeches both entertain and irritate us.

Then finally the announcements are made. We find that Darin Forde has ended up third. He had to surrender some quality trying to keep up with David Fagan. John Kirkpatrick has sneaked past him to take second and the winner for the 10th year in a row is David Fagan. The hall erupts into a standing ovation.

OPPOSITE PAGE: The Father and Sons Competition at the Nationals.

ALAND
AMPIONSHIPS
EXTENDER®
STOCKMA
DB DRAUGHT
DB DRAUGHT
DB DRAUGHT
DB DRAUGHT
DB DRAUGHT

Chapter 7 · AUSTRALIA

Letters From Australia

LETTERS FROM AUSTRALIA

In Wanaka we bumped into the local contractor Colman Rangi. You know when you bump into Colman because he's a big fellow.

In his younger days he played in the front row for Manawatu. Nothing has ever come easily for him and he has come up through the shearing ranks the hard way.

He started out with the intention of becoming a teacher. He attended teacher training college, but changed his mind when he observed the other men who were training to be teachers. "I didn't know if they sat down or stood up when they went to the toilet," he told me.

He has travelled the world shearing, spending several years in Wales. These days he would have probably found himself selected for the Welsh rugby team. In those days he turned out for the village team.

"We used to play little teams in the valleys," he told me. "In Wales you go five kilometres and that's one team, and you go another five kilometres and that's another team. And the tallest guy was usually the fullback because he was the bank manager and he was from England, and the rest of the team were five foot one inches tall, the locks, the props, everybody.

"I must admit that I spent more time watching rugby at Cardiff Arms than I have ever spent watching tests in New Zealand. Every time the All Blacks went there, and they seemed to go about every second or third year in the 70s and the 80s, I was there with thousands and thousands of other Kiwis."

In 1980, Colman and two Maori friends travelled to watch New Zealand play at Cardiff Arms Park for the Welsh centenary test. It was a long trip, driving down from the valleys to Cardiff, but it was even longer getting back. It took them three days! The car broke down, but that wasn't the only reason for the delay. They stopped at every pub on the way.

"The Maori guys' wives just hated me while I was there," Colman said. "We could end up anywhere at any time."

Colman got married and divorced and wandered the world and the shearing sheds until he met his lady, Carol Hyndman.

Originally Carol's father wouldn't let her go into the shearing sheds. But she retained a passion for wool and enjoyed spinning and weaving. She started spinning when she was 14 and bought her first loom when she was 18.

She met Colman while at Massey University getting her wool diploma. He was there doing the same course while convalescing from a shearing injury. By then she too was divorced and their shared passion for wool blossomed into another type of passion.

> **"I always say that what makes a good shearer is poverty."**
>
> **Colman Rangi, shearing contractor**

Nowadays, they have a run based in picturesque Wanaka, but they spent many seasons across the Tasman, chasing the Aussie gold. Most New Zealand shearers do at some point, but few of them come back with as many tales as Colman and Carol.

In Australia you're likely to be in the middle of nowhere, surrounded only by dust and the horizon, working in steaming hot temperatures and with the bare minimum of facilities. As well as spiders and snakes to put up with, there are also the Aussies and the occasional union dispute.

Tales from Oz

The Distance...

Carol: The Flying Cocky

"At one shed way out in the country, the cocky used to fly in from Sydney on Monday and fly home on Friday."

Carol: Happy New Year

"The publican in Hungerford was a great character. Hungerford is about 2000 km from Brisbane. We used to leave the Nissan at a farm about 120 km from his hotel, and when we were heading off to work for the new season, we would always stop there and say hello. When we used to arrive on New Year's Day he would come out to us and he would remember my drink, orange juice – from the year before, and he would have exactly the right beer that Colman drunk and would wish us a Happy New Year."

Colman: The Pub in the Middle of Nowhere

"Hungerford is by the dingo fence and either side of it seems like the end of the world. Every 30 miles or so is a gate that goes through it. It's got the last police station and pub for miles. The only white men in the middle of Australia are the policeman and the publican.

"That publican was an ex-copper. Really his pub was in the middle of nowhere and he turned it into a goldmine. He was an entrepreneur who would bring frozen goods into the desert, things people couldn't normally get there. Everybody went there. Some of them travelled a couple of hundred kilometres just to go to his pub instead of going to their local.

"I remember guys like him because nothing has come to them easy. They not only had to contend with things logistically to get gear there – it was probably a three-day truck trip. Or they would get all the chilled vegetables on a train and then would have to ship them from the stop to where they were – a couple of hundred k's further out. Nothing came easy. When there were floods, they shipped it all by boat. That's just the way they were. No use jumping up and down about it, they just did it."

Getting Your Priorities Right

I was shearing in Wales and the farmer's father died just as we were about to start the shearing season. It was July the 4th and they did the shearing every year at that time. They didn't want to hold up the shearing while they had the funeral so they packed him in ice for a week. They finished shearing the sheep, then they buried him.

Colman Rangi,
shearing contractor

The Facilities...

Carol: Thermal Comfort

"We worked at a shed that was very close to Lightning Ridge in New South Wales. It was about an hour and a half's drive to the thermal pools. We would go there and swim and the warm water used to get rid of all your prickles, aches and pains in your back. It was worth the hour and a half drive over all those roads."

Carol: On the Hot Seat

"The toilets in one shed had metal seats and they faced north. They were side by side and the partition only came down so far. Imagine trying to park your bottom on the metal seats when they had had the sun on them all day. There was no door and no privacy, except you couldn't see the embarrassment on the other person's face."

The Cooks...

Carol: I'm Cooking in the Rain

"Elsie got sick of cooking inside so she cooked bacon and eggs outside in the rain. She just had to go outside because all of us were confined to these little quarters for a month and that's really very hard not to have tempers fray."

Colman: The Queen of Cooks

"The boss put an ad in the paper: 'Wanted, shed hands' and an English girl who was working as a croupier at a casino down in Tasmania applied. When he picked her up she's wearing a dress, sun hat and white gloves like the Queen of England. She came out to the shed and she didn't know one end of a sheep from the other. And she was fantastic. She ended up being our cook and she was turning really good meals out of nothing."

Characters...

Colman: Cloud

"Cloud's English name was Leonard Watt. He was an Aborigine from Western Australia. He was one hell of a boy. Nothing was a problem to him. He came in on one of the dirt roads into the farm on a real wet and muddy night and he cut up the farmer's track. The farmer was going to charge him to fix it up, with a grader and all the rest of it, at a cost of thousands of dollars. In these shearers' quarters they had cans for toilets, and so to make up for cutting up the track, Cloud had to empty the cans. We got a photograph of him afterwards spewing over the fence."

Carol: Winning Lotto

"They won $3.5 million in Lotto and they moved to Western Australia. Mo's wife was very interested in breaking in horses and he bought his wife a big complex in East Ridge. As far as I know he's still shearing. He's not the sort of guy who would let it alter his life."

Colman: Those Who Made It

"There was one chap who shore for 10 years and bought a publishing business. Then there's a boy called Don Smart, we shore with his brother. Don shore for 10 years and in that time he was learning to fly a chopper. I believe he now works flying them. My brother shore for about 15 years and he milks about 600 cows now."

The Wide Comb Wars

In the early 1980s the militant Australian shearing union tried to stop Kiwi shearers using shearing combs that were wider than the ones the Australians used. For a time there was a lot of tension and threats of violence in the industry.

Carol: "The New Zealanders used wide gear and the Australians used narrow gear and there was a big conflict. The Australians reckoned it caused mental illness and a strain to the body using the wider comb and we were shearing more sheep!

"It was a bit like still wanting to drive a Model T car when we've got the nice Toyota to run around in. So the unions were right up in arms about it. We had all sorts of things going on. In one of the sheds we actually had rifles standing at portholes and the instructions were for the female staff to disappear down the porthole in the pens with the sheep and let the men fight the battle upstairs.

"It was scary days really; we weren't safe and we knew we weren't safe. In one shed we worked with a partially Aborigine Australian and he actually had his car burnt in Burke. He had a brand new Ford Falcon and he took it into town to get the stores and the locals actually burnt his car because he was working with

"Never let your daughter marry a shearer. Friday too tired, Saturday too drunk, Sunday too far away."

Anon

Colman in the Front Row

One year a bunch of Kiwi shearers went into the pub and boasted they were going to work on a Saturday morning. So they beat the lot up and left them for dead and the guys that did it to them ended up inside [in prison].

The next year me and Colman went down and sheared at the same shed. Colman was shearing next to the door and he's so big that I thought, "Right if they get past him then I've had it."

So I felt quite safe really.

Mana Te Whata, shearing contractor

Kiwis. One of our shearers had a beer bottle smashed over the back of his head, just being in town at the wrong time."

Colman: "Carol and I were the only ones who never carried a shotgun. They were all loaded ready to go."

More Trouble

Colman: Cancerous Sheep

"These sheep all had cancerous growths. Their heads were absolutely covered in cancer and pus. Just before that time you didn't touch anything cancerous at all. If it came in the yard the shearers would just pack up and go.

"There was about 100 of them and the client wanted most of the wool off them. It was perfectly good wool and wool was more valuable then. So we put sacks on the heads of the sheep and we sheared them for about three times the normal rate. They were killed as soon as they hit the bottom of the deck. The union wouldn't have allowed it. If they'd heard about it, there would have been a scandal."

Carol: Not More Bloody Kiwis

"Colman and I went to work at a shed for Jack Walker in Queensland. Then another shed rang Jack and said they needed a shearer and a shed hand and we were sent. It was a 12-stand shed and when we arrived we went to see the boss to see which was our room and he said, 'Wait a minute, would you mind sitting in the car. We have to take a vote to see if the team will actually work with you.'

"We weren't even allowed to unpack. They never even met us. The team actually went away and voted before we were allowed to join them because we were Kiwis. We had to sit in the car until the vote was finished. And we worked with them for about three years after that, on and off."

Carol: Troubleshooting

"Colman and I were sent down to Commonwealth Hills to do some troubleshooting. The contractor had a gang there, I think it was a 12-stand shed, and he wanted a couple who could go down there and settle the team down. It was a 25-hour car journey from Queensland without stopping, with quick stops if you wanted to go to the toilet, or get something to eat and get straight back in the car.

"In some gangs the personalities just don't hit it off and if you can get a couple of people who are stronger personalities, the weaker ones will tend to hide behind them and the stronger ones know that they have got no power. You just settle the team down; there's no use having this trivial type fighting. We've all got a job to do, that's what our goal is; our goal is not to fight amongst each other. Our goal is to go in and get these sheep shorn and get out of here. So if you have got a couple that think that way you can settle the team down quite well."

Carol: Being Bitten

"I was bitten by a red back spider and I had to spend several weeks in hospital. When I came out the joke went around that I was bitten between holes one and two in the rough on the golf course."

More Aussie Shearing Wars

We worked for one contractor and he'd sit on the roof, and one particular shed we were waiting for these cranks to come and beat us up. We heard the word that they were coming in a big bus load, so he had his bodyguards there and his guard dogs. This guy was packing a 45 and they sat out in front of the gate, but the bus never turned up.

Mana Te Whata, shearing contractor

More Yarning

Carol: What to Do in the Rain

"One time we actually sat in the quarters for a whole month because it didn't stop raining. We couldn't go anywhere or do anything so I taught all the crew to spin. One of the rousies tried to make a jersey for her boyfriend, but she made it so big that they could both fit into it."

Carol: Twilight Yarns

"What do you do in the evenings? It's hot, you'd be looking at I suppose 25 to 37 degrees depending on the range at night and you'd just sit on the flat and have a few beers. We'd just be talking and telling yarns. There's an awful lot of storytelling at night."

The Shearing Life

Carol: Sad Old Men

"Especially in Australia I've worked with some very sad old men who have had everything really. They've had wives, family, children, but here they are in their twilight years and they've got nothing. They don't even know where their family are, a lot of them. They've lost contact or been separated from their wives and they are dominated by the alcohol bottle. They will work all week then spend all their money in the hotel on Saturday, come back to the shed on Sunday night drunk and start work again on the Monday."

Colman: Going Home to Ma

"My father shore for 35 years. When he stopped and stayed home with my mother all hell broke loose. They couldn't live with each other. My mother was used to living by herself. It took them about five or six years to get used to one another again."

Carol: Special People

"You have to be a special person to be in the shearing life. It is hard. There are some days when you ask yourself why the heck do you do it. But it has its rewards. You work hard, but you also have time when you can be independent. You might work every day for four months, but then you might get six weeks off. You don't have that problem of going Monday to Friday for 52 weeks of the year."

HITTING THE ROAD AGAIN

On the Sunday after the open final I returned again to the hall where the Golden Shears had shaken the rafters for the last three days. The door was open and I went inside. The stage, the pens, and the sheep had all gone. Now the hall was empty and very, very quiet.

The shearers and rousies and pressers were long gone – on the road, looking for the next shed and the next sheep. Years ago I wrote a poem about such a life, and by changing just one word I can now dedicate it to all the friends I have made in the shearing sheds.

A wandering shearer I will be,
The winding road appeals to me.
I have no longing for a home,
For my home will be the road I roam.

There is one more thing I want to do before this journey through the shearing sheds of New Zealand is ended. In Romany, the tongue of the international travellers, the Gypsies, I would like to wish all those shearers, rousies, wool handlers and pressers.

"Bahtalo drom"

which means Lucky Road.

BIBLIOGRAPHY

Boards, Blades & Barebellies – Halina Ogonowska – Coates, Benton Ross 1987
The Encyclopaedia of New Zealand Rugby – R.H. Chester and N.A.C. McMillan, Moa 1981
Historic Sheep Stations of New Zealand – Colin Wheeler, Reed 1982
National Geographic Magazine
New Standard Encyclopaedia
New Zealand Sheep and their Wool – Wools of New Zealand
Shearing Magazine
Top Class Woolcutters, The World of Shearers and Shearing – Des Williams, Shearing Heritage Publications 1996.
Wool Away – The Art and Technique of Shearing – Godfrey Bowen, Whitcombe and Tombs 1955

Series consultant: Dr Dorothy Rowe

The author and publisher would like to thank the staff and pupils of the Charles Dickens J & I School, London; the East Leeds Family Learning Centre, Leeds; Mayfield Primary School, Cambridge and Swavesey Village College, Cambridge for their help in making this book

A CIP catalogue record for this book is available from the British Library.

ISBN 0-7136-5052-4

Printed by A & C Black (Publishers) Limited
35 Bedford Row, London WC1R 4JH

Typeset in 15/19 pt Sabon Roman
and 13/19 pt Futura Bold Oblique.

Printed in Hong Kong through Colorcraft Ltd.

CHOICES

I'm Me and You are You

Althea

Photographs by Charlie Best

Illustrations by Conny Jude

A & C Black · London

Everyone is different.

I am tall, so people think I'm older than I am.

I grew up in another country.

I wear glasses, some people tease me.

What is different about you? Does it matter to you?

I wish I had brothers and sisters. There's nobody to play with at home.

There may be things about yourself that you wish you could change.

I wish I had straight hair, then I could grow it long.

I want to cut my pigtails. People pull them, but mum says I look better with long hair.

You can't judge people by the way they look or the way they speak. You need to talk and get to know them.

Janet said she was bullied at her last school. "When I got a brace on my teeth it made my voice sound funny. I was the same person, but people teased me. It made me feel angry and sad inside."

Adrian says that people underestimate him unfairly. "Just because you are different in one way, it doesn't mean you are different in everything. I'm dyslexic but it doesn't stop me playing football."

Being different can be hard. Lots of people are handicapped in some way. Sometimes in ways we cannot see. People who are dyslexic find it very difficult to learn to read or write because they muddle letters like **b** and **d** and they put letters in the wrong order. People sometimes decide that those who have dyslexia must be dim, but they can be very intelligent.

People can be very cruel to someone just because they are different in some way.

Peter says, "My brother is computer mad. He's not that good at talking. Other people think he's odd, and leave him out. He gets very upset."

I'm not good at games and when people pick teams I'm left till last. It hurts and it makes me unhappy. I try to think of other things, like what I'll be doing at the weekend.

The people who live next door to us are cheeky and rude and I don't want to play with them. They say I'm stuck up. They make me feel really small even though I'm older than them.

Cathy says, "Sometimes people get at you just because you are different. Then you start feeling different and they get at you even more. They make fun of my clothes which makes me awkward."

No two people see the world in the same way. The way each of us sees the world comes from our past experience, and no two people ever have the same experience, not even identical twins.

"My brother supports Manchester United but I think they're rubbish. I support Arsenal."

Tom said he thought his life was over when he had to wear glasses and have a patch over one eye. "I tried to pretend I didn't need them but I couldn't see the board. I kept getting the answers wrong. When another boy in the school had to wear a patch he pretended he was a pirate. I wish I had been able to make a joke out of it too."

What really matters is not what happens to us, but how we interpret what happens to us. When Tim got 80% for his spelling test he felt bad because he hadn't got a better mark. When Tim's mum said 80% was brilliant because there were some hard words in the test, Tim was happy.

When people don't understand that other people see things differently, they don't bother to find out how others might be thinking and feeling. As a result they can be very hurtful, especially when they tease.

I had problems with my ears. I had to have cotton wool in them. People thought I couldn't hear. They said nasty things in front of me. It made me very unhappy.

It's good if you can stick up for people who are being teased by pointing out how the person who is being teased feels. But it can be difficult to do it all by yourself.

There was a boy in our class, he had glasses and long hair. He was a loner. I felt really sorry for him, but my friends teased him so I went along with them. I feel really bad about it now. I should have had more courage.

Often people don't want to draw attention to themselves as being different.

Umar says that sometimes people tease him because he is very good at maths. "Sometimes I get it wrong on purpose, but they don't notice and I get bad marks."

Chloe says she tries to pretend she's not scared of heights. "People call me chicken."

Izzy is my best friend. We were in a group who said banana sandwiches were yuck, so we said we hated them too. I love banana sandwiches, then I found Izzy does too! We were just afraid to be different.

Sometimes people may decide not to say what they think because they don't want to upset others.

My friend was so pleased with her new sweater. I didn't tell her I didn't like it.

At times it may be best to keep your thoughts to yourself. Other times it's best to say what you think, even though it may take courage to do so.

When I'm on holiday with my cousin I can't play with my cuddly toys. She's older than me and she makes me feel small. I want to impress her.

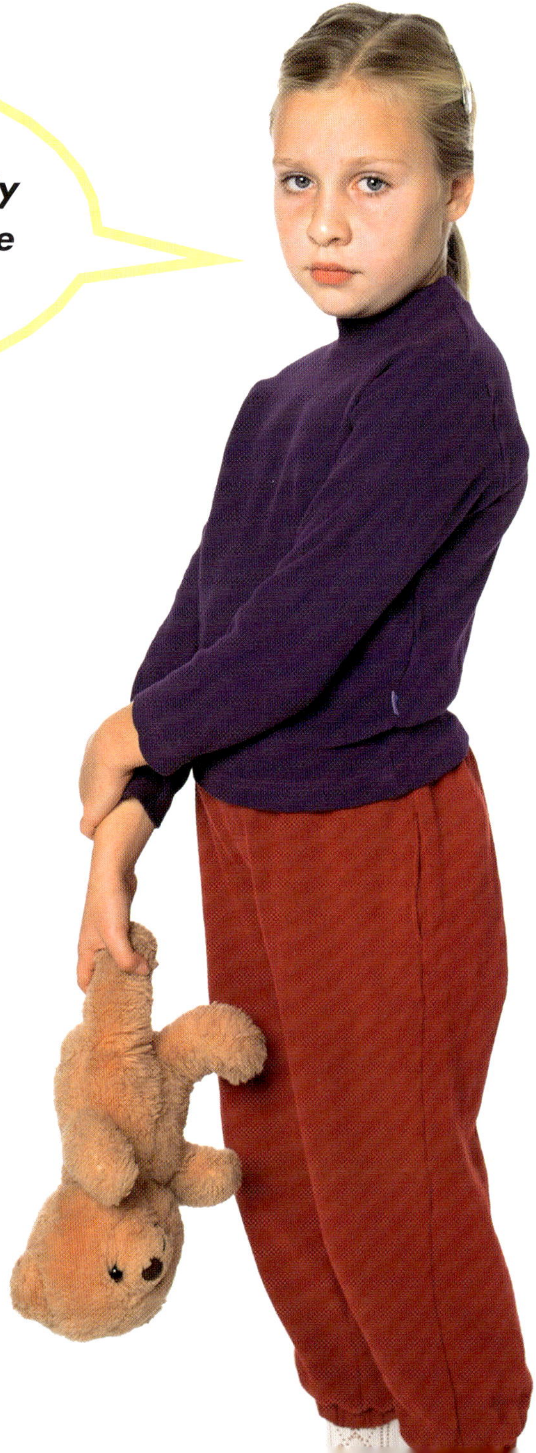

We usually choose friends who seem to see things in the way we do. But it's a good idea to get to know people who see things quite differently from you because you can then learn a lot and have some interesting experiences. You also learn how to make some good compromises.

"My friend and I get on most of the time, but she doesn't like playing the same games as me. She gets grumpy and cries. We make it up by laughing."

It would be bland and boring if everyone was the same.

"I was very fed up when Mum said my cousins were coming to stay. Last time they were silly and messed up all my things. Mum said they're bigger now, so they'll probably be more sensible, but I could put away my best toys just in case."

"In fact they were much nicer and we had a really good time together."

Sometimes you may feel you've grown older than your parents give you credit for.

Rory says he feels frustrated when his friends go skating every Saturday afternoon. "My mum won't let me because she says I'm not old enough to go just with my friends and no adult to mind us. I wish she wouldn't treat me like a baby."

Everyone changes as they grow older and gain more experience. We should try to remain open to change all our lives. Change can be scary, but it always means new opportunities. Kate says her sister started at secondary school last year. "She was really scared at first, but now she loves it. They have a big art department and she goes to drama club. I think I'll like it when I get there."

Misunderstandings often arise because we don't understand how other people think or feel.

"Dad was cross all the time, then he said that I couldn't go to France on the school trip. I thought he was getting at me because I'd had a bad school report. I thought he was being mean and I was horrid to him."

"Later Mum told me he was having a difficult time with work and we really couldn't afford the school trip. That made *me* feel really mean."

Tom says that when his friend Josh broke his pen he was furious. "I thought he had done it on purpose to get at me. He hadn't, he was very upset. I ended up saying sorry to him."

It's always a good idea to ask people what they think and feel because then we don't jump to wrong conclusions.

Sometimes it's difficult for older people to accept differences. Your parents may not agree with your grandparents on the way they think about things. You in turn may not agree with your parents.

Mum was fed up because I won't eat meat. When I talked to her about it and explained how I felt about killing animals she understood. She still finds it annoying having to make me different meals, but I help with the cooking.

We may have been brought up to hold certain opinions. When we talk to others we find they think differently. School is a place where you can learn to get on with lots of people who may hold very different opinions to yourself.

"We should be free to hold different views, as long as we're not harming others by holding these views. In class we have proper debates. The teacher makes us speak in turn and listen to other people speaking. It's good fun and we go on talking about it afterwards. Sometimes we make new friends that way."

Just because people see things differently from you doesn't mean that they're mad or bad. It's just that they have had different experiences from you.

When other people hold different views from you, it doesn't mean that you can't get along with them and treat their views with respect, even though you don't agree with them.

"If you treat their views with respect then you can demand that they treat your view with respect."

If everyone had the same way of seeing things there'd be no point in talking to anyone and life would be very boring. Because everyone is unique life is really interesting.

For teachers and parents

A note from Dorothy Rowe

What determines a person's behaviour isn't what happens to that person but how that person interprets what has happened. No two people ever interpret anything in exactly the same way because no two people ever have exactly the same experience.

When we don't understand that other people can't help but see things differently from us and we assume that we know how another person thinks and feels, misunderstandings soon arise. We can avoid misunderstandings only by knowing that other people see things differently and having good ways of finding out how other people think and feel.

By believing that anyone who thinks differently from us must be bad or mad, we make possible the very worst in human behaviour, from children bullying other children, through racial and religious violence, to war. Children who feel that their views aren't listened to and respected find it very hard to treat other children with tolerance.

Views differ, but not all views are equally valid or useful. Some views cause problems, some are based solely on fantasy, some are misinformed. Through discussions where different views are compared, children can learn how to look at the consequences of the views they hold, and to check their views against reality.

To start a discussion, ask everyone to give an example of how they think they are different to other people in the class. Discuss whether these differences matter.

The following points may be useful when using the book.

Page 3
Discuss the advantages and disadvantages of being an only child. Many children have step parents, and often have experience of both situations. Learning to live with step brothers and sisters takes time.

Page 4-5
When someone has a mental handicap they may find it difficult to communicate. They may not think as fast or seem to react at all at first. Inside they feel just as deeply as other people.

When someone has a handicap it can be difficult to know how much help to offer them. When someone is different in one aspect it doesn't mean they need help with everything.

Pages 6-7
Some people are cruel without meaning to be. They haven't thought through what it must be like to be the other person. How would you feel if you were always left out? Although people learn to cope, it doesn't mean they are happy inside.

Pages 8-9
We can make our lives easier for ourselves by learning to be positive about ourselves and our abilities.

Pages 10-11
People often think teasing is just a bit of fun. They have no idea of how hurtful they are being. Others may tease or bully because they have been bullied themselves. They do it to make themselves feel important.

Page 12
When a whole group appears to think one way, it takes courage to argue. If you do say how you feel you will often find that others will tell you they agree with you, but didn't have the courage to say so at the time. Many adults feel just as shy in a group.

Page 17
Discuss the parent's point of view. Children have to show parents or other adults that they can behave responsibly. Negotiate a compromise - perhaps a parent could come along and remain in the background?

Moving up to secondary school can be quite scary; it may feel to children as if they've become small fish in a big pond. They have to get used to moving from class to class and being taught by different people for each lesson. Children may worry that they won't be able to find their way around.

Pages 18-19
Children may well be able to come up with other examples of when they have behaved unfairly or been treated unfairly through misunderstandings. Discuss how these misunderstandings could have been avoided.

Page 20
This works both ways as children often disapprove of the way their parents behave (smoking being one big issue).

Page 22
Everyone needs to learn to debate and listen to other people's points of view. We can all learn from each other and broaden our outlook.

Further reading

Children may find it interesting and helpful to have a look at some of the following books which also deal with the subject of individuality and people's responses to difference in others.

Rob Childs
Moving The Goalposts
(A & C Black, 1998)

Mick Gowar
The Gang
(Watts, 1995)

Martina Selway
I Hate Roland Roberts
(Red Fox, 1993)

Lynda Waterhouse
Bonnie Fitch
(Red Fox, 1993)